School as a secure base

School as a secure base

How peaceful teachers can
create peaceful schools

Kevin Street

Worth Publishing

First published 2014 by Worth Publishing Ltd
www.worthpublishing.com

Printed and bound in Great Britain by TJ International

British Library Cataloguing in Publication Data
A catalogue record for this book is available from the British Library

ISBN 9781903269237

Text and cover design by Anna Murphy

To Karl Heinz Brisch, and to all who have
taken on the responsibility of bringing
Babywatching to children and young people

NOTES ABOUT THE BOOK

1) To protect the confidentiality of individual children, carers or professionals, names and autobiographical details have been altered in every case quoted. Any case examples written are composite and drawn from a number of similar examples known to the Author from his experiences over many years of working with children and adolescents.

2) To simplify the text, genders are used interchangeably on occasion to represent both male and female pupils, and educational staff. No prejudice implied by this.

3) To simplify the text, the term 'child' has been used on occasion to represent both children and young people. The strategies described are relevant to both primary and secondary phases, unless stated otherwise.

4) To simplify the text, the term 'parent' is used on occasion to represent those now providing the primary care for children and young people. This term will therefore include adoptive parents, foster carers, family and friends.

Acknowledgements

Over many years of teaching I think I must have worked with ten different head teachers, and as we are still very much in a school system that can stand and fall with the heads appointed to lead, I have to firstly acknowledge that their influences - benign, positive, scary, weird, supportive, robust, distant, to name a few - have, over the years, partly shaped how I have come to respond to the pupils in the classrooms and corridors of the schools led by them.

Additionally, there has been a myriad of colleagues, some of whom, from my earliest teaching days, came to represent islands of goodwill and sanity, keeping firm in their commitment to their positive relationships with their pupils, when all around them seemed to be chaotic.

More recently, the education team I led at SWIIS Foster Care worked in an inspired, supportive and good humoured way that brought about changes for the children and young people we worked alongside in ways that were unsurpassed. The team has now been dispersed, but for the support and encouragement we were able to give each other, I have to thank: Sharon, Helen, Sue, Leah, Rob, Marcus, Roz, Aysha, Maria, Donna, Andrew, Manjit and Karen, and from slightly further afield, Julie. Over this time I was particularly helped by the advice and training given by Bridget Betts, especially over issues of attachment, separation and loss. A constant inspiration, due to her own family circumstances that demonstrated time and time again what it is to live with a severely attachment disordered child, and what it was to meet these challenges, was another former colleague, Sandie. Finally, in the decade or so spent at SWIIS, there were scores of children and young people (who teach us as much as they are taught), and their carers, who, on a daily basis, demonstrated the key qualities needed to help these youngsters find a sounder place in life.

Over my life, my own growing belief in the importance of personal peace has been mediated to me by many people - friends, writers, course leaders, speakers - and to all of whom I must express my gratitude. Additionally, I have been very grateful for the insights shared by Carla Hannaford in her writings, and for the work of Heather Geddes, who in a timely and masterly way linked attachment difficulties to problems encountered in the classroom, thus paving the way for a new and vitally important crusade I continue to promote whenever the opportunity arises.

In the process of writing this book, I have been particularly grateful for the time given by Mike Lambert and Patrick Finegan, both head teachers in Dudley (and not included in the roll call above!) And also in the process of writing, I have come to learn the vital importance of an editor who, with skill, patience, humour and empathy, succeeded in allowing my voice to speak - thank you, Andrea Perry. I must also acknowledge the support given to my ideas, enabling this book to be produced, by Martin Wood, of Worth Publishing, and for the creative skill of Anna Murphy in turning raw manuscript into a book that people will be able to read.

Finally, the ongoing encouragement of friends, colleagues, family, and especially my wife, Pam, has sustained me and given me confidence as I produced this book. Thank you!

*A proportion of the royalties from the sale of this book will be donated to BASE®Babywatching UK

ABOUT THE AUTHOR

Kevin Street (BA Hons) PGCE MEd, is a teacher with a wide and varied experience of working with children and young people from Early Years to post 16. He taught English for many years, and was a Faculty Head in a large Nottingham comprehensive school, where he also initiated new schemes of work with students who were on the verge of exclusion.

After some time in Germany, Kevin returned to the classroom as an English teacher in a West Midlands comprehensive school, where he undertook pioneering work in the local authority with Gifted and Talented pupils, as well as teaching Year 7 pupils a broad base of subjects in a project designed to minimise the huge changes between junior and secondary schools.

From there, Kevin started to support the education of Looked After Children, and led a team of teachers and support workers in an independent foster care agency. The children achieved outcomes far in excess of those for their cohort, due to the consistent and informed support the team were able to give, and due to their ongoing advocacy for the children in schools and colleges.

Kevin also trained LAC designated teachers, foster carers and other professionals on the challenges facing Looked After Children in education, especially around issues of attachment.

More recently Kevin has worked in a local PRU, opened a 'pop up' art shop, and is currently a member of the fostering panel for a national charity. He continues to train foster carers, delivers workshops on the theme of peaceful schools, and hosts the Peaceful Schools forum (http://peacefulschools.freeforums.org).

Contents

School as a secure base

Introduction

Look Chloe, I don't care what your reasons are for putting that stuff on your face before the end of my lesson - no, listen, and don't smirk at me like that - you know the rules, and I'm sure that Mr Green would have something to say if - Sabina, don't interrupt, I'm talking to Chloe here - no, I am not shouting, but I will if you don't - Darren! Stay where you are, I need to give you a detention slip for that homework you didn't do - no, you didn't hand it in with the others, don't lie - and don't you shout back at me either - Chloe where do you think you're going? Oi! You lot, don't come in yet, I've not finished with these just wait outside QUIETLY - and so Chloe - no, not you Sabina, you just get off to your next lesson - yes, well Chloe, you should have thought of that before you got the warpaint out - I'm not - what? What did you just say to me? Right that's it - get out, and don't come back - Mr Green will be hearing about this - and pick that book up - Darren? Darren? Come back - OK you lot come in - and don't all rush to the back, just sit quietly - I said QUIETLY - until I've had a word with - Darren? Darren?

Stress, tension, confrontation, a frantic end to one lesson spilling over to the frantic beginning of the next one - and so it piles up, remorselessly, until the exhausted slump in the staff room at the end of another unrewarding day.

Is this how I want to spend the rest of my working life? Is this why I came into teaching? And it's not as if I can walk away from it at the end of the day, with all this new stuff to take on board now with yet more changes to the curriculum.

I feel shattered … changes? Ha! You are joking! It would take a lifetime to change this little lot … wouldn't it? Could things really be any different …?

OK! Well done folks - you all did a good job with this new topic, and we'll pick it up again next lesson. I want you to be in good time for your next lesson, so off you go! Darren and Chloe, can I have a quick word with you both? Alright Sabina, if you have to wait for Chloe, can you just sit down there? Thanks! Now, Darren - you do seem to be having a bit of a problem with meeting these deadlines. Anything I can do to help? Ah - I see - maybe next time let me know a bit sooner? Not to worry, we can sort it out! I'll get a note to your form tutor. OK? Off you go! Now Chloe - oh Chloe, what are we going to do with you? Is it really necessary to top up the tan in lesson time? Come on, be fair - I can't pretend you weren't! Sabina, what do you reckon? Really? That's a bit harsh! Look, it's time you were on your way, and I'll get back to you when I've made life a misery for this next lot! OK, thanks for waiting patiently - in you come, and let's see if we can do even better today than yesterday, and beat the clock for settling down. OK! Coats off, folders out, and let's go for it!

Yes!

This is why I came into teaching - to enjoy the daily contact with young people, to be helpful, inspiring, creative, to give them the best possible start in life.

So how can things change? How we get from A to B? From frantic tension to peaceful security?

Making that journey is the purpose of this book, and it is my hope that by the time you get to the end of it, you will be in a much stronger position, both as an individual teacher and as a member of your school community, to bring about changes that will enhance your work as a teacher and your contribution to creating a secure and peaceful school environment.

But first, let's dig a bit deeper into some of the statistics and facts that make our teaching so challenging and demanding. Let's look at our pupils first.

It seems that each year sees an increase in the depressing statistics of the tensions and challenges faced by children and young people. In his Annual OFSTED Report for 2013(b) on social care, Sir Michael Wilshaw quoted statistics showing that over 700,000 children lived with parents who were overly dependent on

> Think peace, live peace, breathe peace, and you'll get it as soon as you like
> *John Lennon, 1969*

alcohol, and that 130,000 children regularly witnessed domestic violence. These are the children whom we teachers meet daily in school, and who need all the security they can get, even though their behaviour, fuelled by fear, can constantly challenge our attempts to provide this for them.

With determination, though, it's clear that we can create schools that 'hold' insecure and vulnerable children. One shining example was featured in a *TES* article on Duncombe Primary School in North London where 99.6% of all pupils qualify for free school meals, by far the highest number of any school in England; yet by the end of KS2, their results are above local and national averages. As importantly, though, is the fact that the school (meaning of course, the staff, from the head, Barrie O'Shea to the most recent NQT) works in a way to produce the sort of community that remains a sanctuary even for teenagers who have been excluded from school, and who sometimes return to their old primary school for support.

SCHOOL AS A SECURE BASE

"We would rather help than have these children roaming the streets", O'Shea says matter-of-factly, as if any humane school would do the same. *"Sometimes we will have one teenager with us, sometimes it is six. The longest they have stayed with us is three and a half years, and the shortest for one day"*.   *TES* 26.10.12

For a child to feel 'held' (that is, accepted, valued and safely contained), they need to be cared for by staff who are themselves confident, secure and at peace. But is that how the majority of education staff are feeling? Because, on the face of it, the current situation for teachers hardly looks promising, with changes to conditions of service, pensions, yet more exam reform, pressures from SMT to improve results - and all of this before the children arrive in school from the sorts of domestic chaos Sir Michael Wilshaw alluded to in his report (*above*).

Amongst all the things we are asked to focus on, I believe that teachers' well-being has been overlooked and marginalised in the recent decades of heady educational 'reform' in the UK, where new initiatives and new regimes have been piling up, often before full implementation of the previous set. A recent survey of 17,500 teachers (*Teaching Today*, May 2012) recorded that 71% thought that their work had impacted negatively on their well-being, and 97% did not believe that current policies would raise educational standards.

Increasingly, problems at school seem to be having a negative impact on teachers' family life. In the *TES* feature *'Domestic bliss? Far from it'* (8.2.13), the Teacher Support Network reported that 80% of all the calls it gets are about concerns over well-being and family relationships, and a survey ran by this charity in 2011 recorded that 96% of

> Peace cannot be kept by force; it can only be achieved by understanding
> *Einstein, 1930*

respondents thought that their home life was being affected by their workload at school. In an NUT survey conducted in January 2013, 55% of the 800 teachers surveyed reported that their morale was low or very low. Survey after survey returns a similar picture, until we come to the most disturbing one of them all - the figures relating to teacher suicides, surely the ultimate cry of distress. In the UK between 2006 and 2009, (the most recent figures available) there was an increase of 80% of teachers taking their own lives, from 35 to 63 - in other words, the staff of a medium sized school (*TES* 1.6.12). This is about 40% higher than the national average for people within similar occupations (for example, law or medicine).

Peace is a daily, a weekly, a monthly process, slowly eroding old barriers, quietly building new structures
John F Kennedy, 1963

Doom and gloom indeed. But I believe that despite all the turbulence of educational change, it is possible for us to regain a deep sense of our real purpose as educators, teachers, guides of children.

> Reform seems to be starting with an incorrect assertion that teachers are the problem; instead … teachers are the solution.
>
> Mike Brilland, *Guardian Professional* 12.6.12

Others, too, echo the need for teachers to regain this central role:

> Create a genuinely high status profession who are seen not as part of the problem but as part of the solution.
>
> Brian Lightman, *The Independent* 10.9.11

WAYS FORWARD?

In a form of self fulfilling prophecy, it has to be said that sometimes we teachers can indeed become a problem - disgruntled, threatened, stressed and dissatisfied, generally feeling besieged. It is this that I particularly want to address. Because if we feel we can only perform well in a stress-free environment, with enhanced pay and conditions, anticipating a pension that reflects the contribution we have really made over the years, in buildings that are always fit for purpose and beyond, backed by a sympathetic and supportive government - we are, I think you'd agree, going to wait for a long, long time.

The other side of the equation - the pupils we get - was well addressed by a leading Finnish educationalist, Pasi Sahlberg. Commenting on the envy with which the world looks at his country's achievements, he directed our gaze away from the system, and said:

> I think a lot of this success comes from parents and communities outside school ... (Finnish students) are happy and healthy and secure and loved kids, most of them. If you have that kind of privilege in your society it's no wonder that things go well.   *TES* 1.11.13

Realistically, I think we are equally going to be waiting a long time for our pupil population in the UK to reflect this ideal as well.

Of course this isn't new news. But when stress is high, it's all too easy to believe that if government, or the head teacher, or pupils' behaviour were different, then the situation would improve of its own accord. In an attempt to address the challenge of stress, a number of initiatives have emerged over the recent years to encourage schools to become more peaceful - conflict resolution, anger management, restorative justice, school coaching, to name a few. Although these have their role to play, I believe that until the core issues are addressed, *concerning our own sense of peace and conscious reduction of stress as teachers*, such schemes will be of limited value. The reduction of this stress, and the introduction of personal peace and calm into our lives as teachers, is the way forward that I am pursuing in this book.

Is peace, though, just an absence of conflict? In today's schools, even such an absence might be a rare treat, as all the partners in the educative process seem to be forever sparring - government, unions, heads, inspectors, parents, teachers, support staff - and in amongst it all, our pupils.

When I asked for their definition of peace, a number of teachers suggested the following:

Image 1: How do you define peace in school?

Out of these a state emerges that might be something like this:

> "I feel a sense of trust and calm contentment, and I feel that I can see the reality of the whole picture. From this sense of wholeness, I feel that I can move on, and can engage with my pupils from a position of confident strength".

SCHOOL AS A SECURE BASE

Ah! Would that we could gain such an inner strength, one that enabled us to approach everything we encounter on our daily journey from Period One to Period Five - and beyond - with an assurance that carries all before it, and results in amazing outcomes for all concerned.

In common with so many teachers, my career has taken some interesting turns, none more so than the most recent when I taught for a term in a local PRU. Faced with teenagers for whom 'the system' no longer held any kudos (they'd been through it all, done it all, and refused point blank to wear any T Shirt not of their choosing), I had to draw on every ounce of my own inner strength and sense of well-being to see me through the day, and whilst the outcomes were not always easy to see, we got along pretty well in a teaching situation that could often seem surreal. Certainly, one of the keys I used was to avoid confronting the students aggressively and to try to allow them to feel relaxed in the classroom.

There is overwhelming evidence that behaviour and learning flourishes when pupils are relaxed and not charging around fuelled by an excess of adrenaline. The key to this relaxation partly rests in the environment - in our classrooms, corridors, playgrounds, dining halls, toilets, in everything that makes up 'the school'.

But of course we need to go further than this. Environments don't just happen. They are created by those who are in a position to influence them the most - us, the teachers who form the heart of any and every school. And a healthy heart bodes well. But an *unhealthy* heart brings stress, strain, and breathlessness, all the symptoms many of us might recognise from the end of Year 11 General Studies last lesson on Friday, or from the last 'Golden Hour' of our class day when we are feeling anything but golden!

If you cannot find peace within yourself, you will never find it anywhere else
Marvin Gaye, songwriter - musician, 1939 - 1984

So - as teachers we had better start to value our well-being, and to learn what we *can* do, rather than fretting about what we can't change. What we can do is to change our reactions to situations, to change what has become a knee jerk, habitual response to a challenge, and to stop, take stock of ourselves, and realise that we can provide our own answers to the problems that seem to surround us.

Peace comes from within, do not seek it without
Gautama Buddha

Is this harsh? Maybe, but consider Leo Tolstoy when he writes:

Everyone talks about changing the world, but nobody talks about changing themselves. *Three Methods of Reform*, 1900

In a similar vein, but starting to get beneath the surface of what our task is in the quest for peace, Eckhart Tolle (2003) advises:

You find peace not by rearranging the circumstances of your life, but by realising who you are at the deepest level.

I suppose it is ultimately this quest to 'find ourselves' that lies at the heart of what I am suggesting in *School as a Secure Base*. Teaching is a calling, it is a vocation, and one that depends ultimately on the dynamic between us and our pupil, two human beings bringing to each encounter a lifetime of experiences, all of which have moulded the quality of that moment.

And in that moment, I might expect the adult, ourselves, to have due regard not only to the background of the pupil, but to our own background, to those life events that are making themselves felt as the encounter between us plays out. Not that I'm expecting in any realistic way that such a continuous stream of self-analysis will punctuate each encounter of the school day - that way lies madness!

What I am advocating though is a willingness on our part to start on a process that will inevitably lead to this type of reflection as a natural part of our day. It is one that will provide a firm, secure foundation that will enable any of us to take far greater control of our working lives. In doing this, I really believe that we will create schools that are more secure, peaceful and nurturing than we could ever have imagined possible!

So in **Section One,** I will address the core issue of **Bringing Peace to Teachers** as we track the progress of one teacher from a horrendous Period One on a Monday to a calm last day of term, looking at ways in which we can start to find our own inner core of peace.

If, as I believe, we teachers are the most important link in this process, pupils are easily a close second, so **Section Two** turns to highly effective ways of **Bringing Peace to Pupils.** But wait a minute - what if - that's fine for you, but … **Section Three** scripts the exchange that took place between myself as a front-line teacher (and well-meaning author), and a very savvy head teacher, whose experience was enough to fill at least one bucket of cold water. In answering his questions and challenges about the ideas I had put forward about creating a peaceful school, I found myself thinking sharply about some of the realistic and inevitable challenges my suggestions would throw up, and how these reasonable objections could be countered. I'm grateful to him for such an honest and helpful interview!

Section Four moves on into techniques that can help us in **Bringing Peace to Classrooms**, regardless of whether we find ourselves in a new purpose-built learning environment or a way past its sell-by date mobile classroom on the edge of the field. Moving out from the classroom, **Section Five** addresses what is needed when **Bringing Peace to Schools,** exploring playgrounds and beyond. Finally, in **Back to the Beginning, Section Six** charts what has been achieved, and how we can move forward.

The centrality of the teacher/pupil relationship is critical to all this, and either of the two images below can serve as a working model for what I am going to look at further. But my central point remains that unless we as teachers are at peace with ourselves and in ourselves, our working life will be compromised, and school will not be a secure base either for us or for our pupils.

So, here's how I think of this in simple diagrammatic form

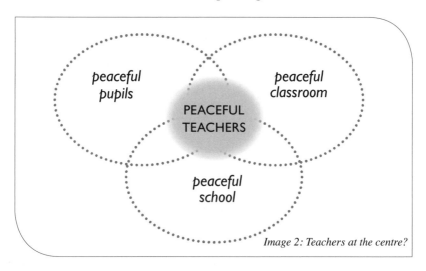

Image 2: Teachers at the centre?

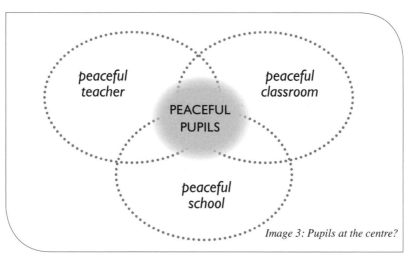

Image 3: Pupils at the centre?

SCHOOL AS A SECURE BASE

We might want to argue chicken and egg over these two - which comes first? My aim is to show you how central you are and how much influence you can exert, for the better, whatever else is going on around you. So I maintain that as teachers are central to the whole process of creating security and peace, *Image 2* represents this best. We remain the lynchpin to the whole concept of schools being and becoming places where the security, peace and well-being of all is the basic foundation of everything that follows.

And once both these models are in place, we can finally look forward to our peaceful school: *Image 4*.

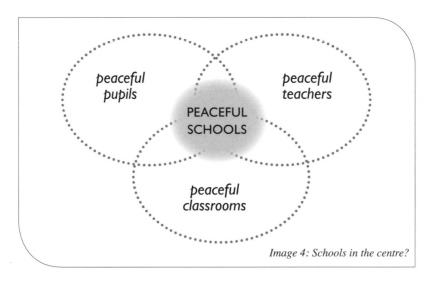

peaceful
pupils

peaceful
teachers

PEACEFUL
SCHOOLS

peaceful
classrooms

Image 4: Schools in the centre?

In the creation of secure, peaceful schools, in which pupils feel 'held' (*see* p.4), their basic needs will be recognised and met. They need to feel that they are:

- ✓ Valued and respected for who they are.
- ✓ Safe in class and around the school.
- ✓ Relaxed in knowing that their best interests are being protected.
- ✓ Happy to explore new ideas and take risks.

And supporting this are us, their teachers, whose actual needs are not very different from those listed above, apart from our ongoing need to review and reflect on how we can continually enhance and enrich what ultimately makes us 'tick'.

> There is only one corner of the universe you can be certain of improving, and that's your own self.   Aldous Huxley, 1944

It is the process of 'improving' ourselves that Huxley mentions, that will be the basis of Section One, *Bringing Peace to Teachers*.

SCHOOL AS A SECURE BASE

Section one
BRINGING PEACE TO TEACHERS

'Physician, heal yourself!'

This saying points to an ancient wisdom: that any practitioner must be able to practise the best of their art on themselves before they turn to helping others. I am more likely to take the advice of my doctor to lose a few pounds and take up exercise if this particular GP isn't overweight and clearly out of breath from seeing me to his surgery door!

As teachers, we want the best for our pupils at all levels. We want to see them achieve their academic potential, but we also want to see them thrive as human beings. There might be ulterior motives in this - I am reminded of the slogan: *'Be nice to your children - they are the ones who will choose your nursing home!'*

Of course part of what makes us teachers is recognising that children are our future. We can teach subjects and skills, but there is so much more than this. We teach children and young people through who we are and what we do and how we relate to them, and the examples we set will either serve to reinforce negative images of the adult world, or challenge and inspire our pupils to do their best.

It is perhaps the enormity of our task that makes some teachers flippant about the effects they have on their pupils. I believe they underestimate the impact we can have as teachers on a child's life. The way we approach our classes on a daily basis, the attitudes we hold towards all our pupils, the quality of our interactions with children in and out of the classroom - all of these are seen by our pupils as pointers to our own authenticity as people, whether we really do 'practise what we preach'. I can't expect a pupil to improve her spelling if my comments on her work are shoddy and misspelt; I can't expect a class to feel enthusiastic about Shakespeare if I am struggling to find pleasure in his work; and I can't expect my pupils to adopt a calm, relaxed and positive attitude to learning if I am on edge, ill at ease and negative.

This is the reason why I know that central to a peaceful school are peaceful teachers, and that if we can grasp this and make it our own, we can change the atmosphere and outcomes in the schools where we teach.

So from this section, you will ...

✓ Understand the central role of the teacher in creating a peaceful, secure school.
✓ Realise why 'behaviour packages' don't last.
✓ Start to think about how you think.
✓ Learn simple techniques to become peaceful.
✓ Acquire the skills to start your own support network.

The central role of the teacher in creating a peaceful school

The big squeeze

Over the last 30 years teachers have been expected:

- to deliver a curriculum not of our making
- to interact with our pupils in ways that reflect changing notions of correctness
- to submit to increasing levels of external scrutiny
- to take responsibility for a school system not of our making

It is small wonder that in a recent survey, 52% of teachers were actively seeking to leave the profession (NAS/UWT survey, May 2012), and 55% of those surveyed in an NUT January 2013 poll reported that their morale was low or very low. We might expect at any time there to be discontent 'within the ranks' of whatever profession is surveyed, but this figure points to a discontent and unhappiness that should not be ignored. For even if our colleagues don't or can't leave, their whole outlook and discontent can permeate our schools and classrooms.

Whatever the effects of a curriculum that fails to meet pupils' needs, or whole school policies that are clearly unrealistic and out of tune with 21st century reality, the daily grind of uncomfortably disciplined classrooms has ranked high for stressed teachers. New research from the EU published in 2012 (conducted by the the Freiburg Research Centre for Occupational and Social Medicine, questioning 5,400 teachers in 500 schools across Europe) has indicated that teachers in the UK experience some of the following factors in our classrooms.

UK teachers:
- had the highest levels of burnout
- had the second highest levels of cognitive stress
- had above average levels of lesson disturbances
- had higher than average levels of verbal abuse and conflict with parents
- and scored second lowest in terms of the influence they felt they had in the workplace

A strong and consistent picture emerges of a workforce that is far from content, and in desperate need of personal support. An anonymous teacher contributing to a *TES* column entitled *'What keeps me awake at night'* (14.9.12) wrote:

> When Sir Michael Wilshaw said that teachers don't know what stress is, he misread his notes: they do not know what safe stress is - the energising, invigorating stress that leads to creative problem solving. I'll say yes to that, but no to the stress that pushes people towards ill health and even suicide.

I would question even this first definition of stress, as ultimately stress is never 'safe', but can too easily spill over into negatively affecting health and well-being, leaving some of our colleagues in extreme peril.

Hammers aren't the answer

Poor behaviour in schools shows little sign of abating. On March 30th 2012, the *Daily Telegraph* reported that the Association of Teachers and Lecturers claimed pupils were being allowed to run wild with a 'total disregard of school rules', with half of their members saying that behaviour had worsened in the last two years. A little later, in July of the same year, Barnado's, in a press release ahead of a Channel 4 documentary entitled *Lost Children,* took a slightly different slant on bad behaviour. They warned that schools needed to do more to tackle the root causes of bad behaviour, and their Chief Executive, Anne Marie Carrie stated: *"A school teacher's job is not an easy one, but they must look behind the behaviour to see the child. Unruly pupils may be acting out, not just acting up".*

For many years a plethora of solutions and packages have been handed down. More recently, the 'zero tolerance' approach has been imported from the USA, intended as a tough response to pupils' indiscipline. One example of verbal abuse, and the pupil is 'out'.

However, this is so often like sticking a plaster on a festering cut without properly cleansing the wound. Sooner or later infection returns, often more virulently than before. My own experience in supporting the education of Looked After Children has confirmed this on many occasions, with the child, on an exclusion, experiencing yet more adult 'rejection' for acting in a way that is so embedded in their survival mechanism it would take years of patient hard work to reverse (*see pp.*83-93).

This is what Barnado's was referring to in July 2012. But for teachers who have little or no support in understanding this type of behaviour, the recourse to exclusion is understandable. For the teacher, under stress from a variety of other sources, a foul-mouthed truculent pupil is the last thing they need.

Some years ago, I was in exactly this position with one Year 9 lad who suddenly appeared in a class I had just 'succeeded' in calming, to disrupt and agitate until he disappeared a few weeks later just as suddenly. I had not dealt with him appropriately. But back then I knew nothing of the educational problems of Looked After Children, and blindly followed the 'usual' disciplinary routes. The course I had attended earlier that term, on rewarding positive behaviours, was totally ineffective with this boy, and left me questioning the whole value of such strategies. And, it has to be admitted, left me also questioning my own effectiveness.

It made me realise then, as it does now, that the days of 'bolt on' courses on managing behaviour are numbered.

> Training events led by charismatic behaviour consultants may be highly entertaining and inspirational, but they can leave some teachers feeling inadequate because they could never, in a million years, imagine themselves being able to exude such 'personality capital', confidence and prowess when dealing with challenging behaviour.
>
> Derrington & Goodard 2007, p.5

On the one hand, the 'Behaviour Package': on the other hand, the classroom/ school. It seems as if 'all we need to do' to join them is to simply attach a teacher.

But if that teacher is under strain, weakened by other events, or is discontent and unhappy, it won't be long before the 'Behaviour Package' sheers off, leaving the teacher feeling more disempowered and ineffective than ever, and seeking to lay the blame on pupils, parents and politicians. And whilst we are in the land of B&Q analogies, we might hear Maslow's assertion:

> If the only tool you have is a hammer, you tend to see every problem as a nail.
>
> Maslow 1966

As teachers, we need a range of tools to bring about change, and hammering away out of habit will no longer bring results, only frustration and fatigue. If teachers are going to use new tools, we need training and confidence in their use, and this is where we can look to *the teacher as a person as the main force for change.*

In a paper on educational reform (2004) by Elizabeth Hinde, from the University of Arizona East, the work of J Fullan is mentioned. Fullan (1997) lists the three most common reasons for the failure of new education initiatives:

- Teachers are alienated
- The most reform-minded teachers are 'burnt out'
- There are too many fragmented, unconnected initiatives

This has also been recognised by Professor John Hattie, one of the most controversial figures in world education. Over the last twenty years he has compiled possibly the most extensive piece of research ever conducted into what works best in the classroom, and as a result he has become highly critical of teacher training, as not delivering the things that matter.

What these 'things' are soon becomes evident on reading his book, *Visible Learning* (2008), which draws on the experiences of eighty million pupils across the English speaking world. Of the one hundred and thirty six most effective classroom interventions he lists, the most effective ways to raise the standard of education are *to raise the quality of the interactions between teachers and their pupils, and to raise the quality of feedback pupils get from teachers.* This is despite, much to his surprise, the fact that issues over homework, class sizes and type of school which appear low down on his interventions list, '… still dominate our debates. We like to talk about the things that really don't matter.' (John Hattie in an interview with the *TES,* 14.9.12).

Time and time again the message that *It's all about the teaching* comes through, but despite the fact that Hattie's work has been in circulation now for over ten years, it seems that it is only recently that there is an attempt to translate the findings into classroom practice (for example, through the training offered by 'Visible Learning Plus(™)' - *see Appendix 1*). It would of course be interesting to see whether the basic tenets of Hattie's evidence - that teachers and their classroom practice are central to real change and improvement - are ever paired with the means to genuinely offer teachers the capacity to reflect and change.

If the interaction between us and our pupils is to be enhanced, as teachers we need to be in a space that enables us to draw on our own inner resources, since we can be sure that the external influences on education aren't going to change overnight.

And what are these inner resources? The breathless nature of some teaching post adverts can start the ball rolling, since candidates are often urged to display 'a good sense of humour', 'high levels of energy', 'personal drive and a passion for education', 'dynamism', 'vision', 'creativity', 'excellent inter-personal skills', 'inspiration' - the list goes on, and would seem to be at odds with the surveys I referred to earlier on.

Yes - if only all these qualities could be produced in the twinkling of an application form, and maintained as the realities of the new post begin to bite. Of course we all know colleagues who seem to draw on reserves of strength and power to whirl them with passionate enthusiasm from one lesson to the next, leaving the question *"Just what is she on?"* in their wake. But are the qualities of warmth, excitement and positivity the preserve of a select few, or can they be the wellspring for many teachers?

I really believe that if we place ourselves at the centre of the educative process, and our well-being as a priority, we can start to experience (or re-find) the excitement and enthusiasm that needs to underpin our work with children and young people. At the very heart of this is our own self-confidence, our own feeling of self-worth, and our conviction that we have the skills necessary to make a difference in the lives of those we teach and influence.

Just as there are no 'bolt on' quick fix courses to manage pupil behaviour, there are no quick fix ways to boost our own inner resources. But it is possible for teachers to enjoy all of the qualities mentioned in the adverts, if we take ourselves seriously - though paradoxically, the suggestions I will be making throughout this book can be anything but serious, as heavy dullness has no place in our inner life.

At the core of what I am describing is our own sense of peace, of calm, of a joyful confidence that will not only enhance our teaching, but will give us wings to fly high in all aspects of our lives. The rewards are rich and wonderful! - if we recognise ourselves and our own well-being as our most precious resource, and take care of ourselves accordingly.

A path to peace

Lysander	He hath rid his prologue like a rough colt; he knows not the stop. A good moral my lord; it is not enough to speak, but to speak true.
Hippolyta	Indeed, he hath played on this prologue like a child on a recorder - a sound but not in government

From 'A Midsummer Night's Dream'
William Shakespeare

Oh dear! The above conversation between two members of the audience of a play being performed by a bunch of ham-fisted amateurs highlights what goes wrong when words are spoken without a real understanding as to what lies behind them. The lesson we can take from it is also apt - that to simply learn a 'script' to promote good behaviour won't work unless it is a part of our core beliefs. We can learn the words, but they won't necessarily be in the right order.

The aim of this Section is to encourage all educational staff to become peaceful. If we can do that, all our work will be underpinned by peace. The words that we speak and the examples that we give will be grounded in quiet confidence. What would that look like, in practice?

SCHOOL AS A SECURE BASE

✓ The classroom becomes a focus of real learning and cooperation. Pupils feel confident that their teacher can keep them safe, and that they can take risks in their learning. The atmosphere is light, good humoured and positive. Whatever a pupil presents, they feel held and secure. They recognise that they are valued and respected, and the teacher is able to draw on individual strengths to help overcome individual weaknesses.

✓ The playground is a place of fun and safety, enabling all pupils to relax in ways they find appropriate. Staff on duty engage positively with the children, whilst ensuring extremes of behaviour are managed.

✓ Staff meetings are chances to explore, challenge, listen and grow. Staff feel supported and valued by all their colleagues.

✓ Support staff, whether in classrooms, offices, kitchens, libraries or playgrounds are respected by teaching colleagues and pupils. Their contribution to the happiness and smooth running of the school is acknowledged and valued.

✓ Challenging situations - and yes, of course they will happen in classrooms, playgrounds and staff meetings - will be met at the right level by staff who are confident in their understanding of the situation, and confident in themselves as human beings. Whilst not tolerating disrespect, they realise that their worth can never be undermined by 'the other', and will act in a way that defuses, not enflames, the situation.

Being part of the 'solution', teachers are central to whatever solution the problems demand, and to try to solve anything without teachers on board is going to fail. We are our own, and in many senses our only, best starting point.

> We need to be the change we wish to see in the world.   Gandhi

Once again, timeless advice that places the responsibility of change on the shoulders of each of us as individuals. As indicated in the Introduction, what constitutes 'peace' varies, but I'd really like to make one thing clear. A peaceful teacher is not someone coasting in neutral, in a haze of fuzzy good intent, but one who can assert:

> *"I am confident, prepared and have the ability to communicate successfully with my classes, in a way that will bring about real learning."*

Flexibility, interest, a sense of humour and an ability to stay calm are all a part of this, but might not come naturally to many of us, at least not at first. Most of us come into teaching with some degree of altruism, keen to make a difference, but initial training, and subsequent INSET, often leave us without the ongoing support to develop the additional techniques which I believe are crucial if we are to become teachers who work out of a deep sense of inner worth.

Our own 'baggage', those life experiences that have moulded us into who we think we are, naturally come into play. For those who are 'glass half full' people, this 'baggage' might be helpful; but for those who are 'glass half empty' people (and that's on a good day!), the daily challenges of the job can soon take their toll.

What I am suggesting is this: that in order to discover within ourselves those qualities that will underpin our well-being and success as teachers, we need to take time to pause and to reflect on just *why we react in the classroom in the way we do,* and how this might be changed for the better, whilst still remaining true to ourselves. There is nothing wrong with our 'baggage' as long as we are totally sure that it is still necessary for our journey - and that we are aware who packed the bag in the first place!

New ways forward

> The only person you can control is yourself, so practise self-calming
> skits.   Victor Allen, in the *TES* 24.8.12

I'm well aware how some teachers may view the central tenet of this Section -
that the key to change is in ourselves. I can sympathise with anyone who turns
and politely informs me what I can do with this way of thinking - that they
have enough to cope with in life and work without being told that it's us who
needs to change. So what am talking about - the introduction of yet more DoE
brainwashing?

The truth is the exact opposite to external interference or directive. That
until we can pause, stop and really examine *what we think and why we think it*,
we are going to be pulled in all directions by thoughts and reactions that possibly
have no further place in our lives, even if they did at one time.

I imagine I may be skating on thin ice by addressing weary teachers at the
end of another long day and suggesting that we embark together on a journey of
self-examination, or add to our current discomforts by confronting the things that
'makes us tick', in the pursuit of inner peace. But my experience has shown me
that there really is no other way forward if teaching, learning, and the security of
our future generations is to be underpinned by a profession that is confident and
inspired. So in this chapter I will be exploring just a few of the proven ways that
have been helpful in enabling people to gain a deep sense of peace and security
that can underpin their life and work.

Of course, there are hundreds of titles, courses, gurus, CDs, and therapies
that can all help in this process, their suitability dependant on the taste and
attitudes of the one who seeks them out. Added to this are the great religions
of the world, the philosophies and theories, that have actually stood the test of
time. Somewhere, in the world supermarket of truth, there will be the right

'product' for you, and there are plenty of consumer guides to help in that choice well beyond the scope of this book.

However, what I will be doing here is to present some techniques of which I have had personal experience, and which have been shown to work, especially in an educational setting.

Supporting these approaches is science. The days of the duality that has been forced between 'science' and 'belief' should now be over, as neuroscience and quantum theory show us that we are more than just clever machines. We are key stakeholders in the created order, well able to influence many aspects of our lives in ways that only recently would have been deemed 'psychobabble'. I'll look at some of these processes later, when describing practical and peaceful ways of helping contain disturbing behaviours.

A school visit

Before we set off on this process of opening our own doors to peace, I would like to take you through a process from the beginning of a Monday morning to the end of term. These stages will be marked by a number of poems that chart the process for an individual teacher - but if poetry isn't your 'thing', you can skip them and read the bits in between - and be reassured that no teachers were harmed in the writing of this section! At least, no more than usual …

The school we are visiting is Any School - neither 'outstanding' nor 'in need of improvement', and the pupils at the school are not deliberately malicious. Even Darren, the protagonist we meet later on, is not hardened in his surliness, but reacts in a way any teen might who feels he has to save face in front of his mates. The teacher is struggling though; tired, feeling undermined in his work by one 'initiative' after another, and what joy he once felt for teaching has been replaced by a dull apathy and hopelessness.

SCHOOL AS A SECURE BASE

And so - the bell rings, and Period One, Monday morning, starts...

FIRST THINGS

Discover my truth?
S'truth,
What are you on about?
It's 8.55 on a Monday
And spilling out of their weekend
Is my Year 11
Boasting, bragging
Calling, crowing
Think they're it
And it's showing!

Can I get anywhere near
Beneath bravado's veneer
And scratch their inflated bubble
Make them value learning?
Ha! That's a laugh!
What do they care for me, my way
All I have to say - washed away.

How dare you speak to me
Like that!
How dare you sneer and laugh
Like that!
Get outside
Go on - get out
And stay out!

That tight knot
That fear
That dry-mouthed, pounding fear
That gut-wrenching panic
That my core is in meltdown
No foundations left

To support me as I fall
Shaking as I stumble
To the door
Clawing to be out
With empty laughter
And wasted notes
Strewn across the desks
Behind me.

And you talk to me
About truth.
My truth?
My story?
And all that's left
Is this wreck
Washed up, mangled
Shredded already

With 19 time-slotted
Agonies left until Friday.

This is fiction - poetic fiction at that - but from my own experience I know that it captures, in concentrated form, the ripples and surges of anxiety so many of us and our colleagues in school feel from time to time - and for some, for much of the time. Talking about his working life deteriorating beyond measure, a teacher identified as 'Mark' in a *TES* article on stress (1.6.12) wrote of the 'leaden limbs' and 'nauseous churning stomach' at the start of every day, of fear and hopelessness, with symptoms getting increasingly worse:

> *"I wandered round the school on legs of treacle, with less and less to say to anyone. The noise in my classroom was rising steadily by the day; not of course the noise of creative learning but the noise of the mob that was increasingly rampant".*

Contemplating suicide, Mark instead suffered a breakdown, but with counselling returned to the classroom, and has since become a dedicated and effective teacher.

Life in school can be seen as a daily battle, a conflict of different interests as students pull one way and their teachers the other. Such daily confrontations don't seem to wear down the students though, although clearly such repetitive angst and high emotion will be having some effect: but it is staff who are very obviously run ragged. And this is not new: D H Lawrence's brief experiences as a teacher inspired a vivid evocation of this same state in his poem *Last Lesson*, opening with the memorable line:

When will the bell ring and end this misery?   1912

However, I don't wish to linger any longer on the negative. I want to start now to unravel the strands that will bring teachers peace.

THE CHALLENGE

If you can't
Teach an old dog
New tricks
Then why did Goethe bother to write:
We must always change, renew, rejuvenate ourselves; otherwise we harden.

If a leopard
Can't change
Its spots
Then why did Zangwill point out:
Things do not change; we change.

So - which side of the divide
Do you stride?
Are you ready and willing

To haul up your habits
By the boot string of
Self-examination?

To look long and hard
At why you do?
At how you do?
At what you do?
OR -
Retreat into a cave
Of shell like denial
Too much of a trial
To think anymore?

I would like to invite you to start to consider a few ways that can really help to establish a core of peace that will underpin your teaching in a positive way, and leave you feeling energised and in control - of yourself, of your classroom, and of your working day. I will be looking at several different techniques.

- ✓ Thinking about the way you think
- ✓ Peer mentoring
- ✓ Writing it all down - keeping logs and lists
- ✓ Taking personal responsibility
- ✓ Professional support
- ✓ Heart coherence
- ✓ Using sensory space
- ✓ Persistence
- ✓ Humour

I will explore these in the next part of this chapter, starting with the invitation to look into your own mind and ways of thinking. But I suggest that before we start, it's important to touch base with where we are actually 'at' in this very moment.

Take a deep breath and ...

If I were a stage hypnotist, I would ask you to look deep into my eyes and start to feel sleepy - but don't worry! Nothing alarming is about to happen. Before we start on the process of examining what we do and why we do it, it is important that we are in a good physical space to begin with. The following check list may help:

- ✓ Are you really sitting comfortably?
- ✓ What about your physical posture? Are your shoulders raised or relaxed? Are you involuntarily holding your breath? Are you clenching any part of your body? Where is your tongue?
  A few pointers towards relaxation: shoulders lowered, all parts of your body at ease, exhale a few times, tongue resting in the floor of your mouth, not touching the roof ... - and yes - yawn!
- ✓ Clothing - not too tight ... ?
- ✓ Comfortable warmth ... ?
- ✓ Do you need a drink - water, tea, a *small* glass of something ... ?
- ✓ You've had something to eat ... ?
- ✓ Is your phone off ... ?
- ✓ And perhaps a walk round the block if events of the day are still crashing around inside you ... ?

You might also have additional ways of relaxing, and if so, do whatever you need to bring yourself into readiness for this next section.

Crunch time! What do you need to change?
Thinking about the way you think

> Whether you think you can or think you can't, either way you are
> right.   Henry Ford, 1863-1947

Ford's enigmatic statement pre-dates a growing 21st century understanding - that thought and thinking are powerful processes that can shape our experiences of the world in very real ways. What is known as *metacognition* is the basic expression of this, the process of taking time to actually analyse our thinking, and the habits we have picked up over the years. The foundations of our thinking are laid in our earliest years and the experiences we have of the world.

As educators we are very aware that the children and young people we see on a daily basis have already had significant social conditioning before they ever start school, and that if this has been traumatic, a catalogue of abuse and neglect, the neural pathways in their brains might actually be hardwired very differently to those in a child whose upbringing has been consistent and loving (*this is explored at greater length in Section Two, Bringing Peace to Pupils* pp.77-9, 87-92). The reputed claim of the Jesuits - '*Give me a child until he is seven and I will give you the man*' has echoes here, and our attempts to modify the most harmful excesses of poor social conditioning can often seem still-born, unless we address this issue.

However, if this is true for children, it has also been true for us. The surprise young children have at seeing 'Miss' shopping with her partner and her

33

own children can be amusing, but the notion of the teacher as a one-dimensional figure who is wheeled out of the cupboard at the start of each school day is at times confirmed by pigeon-holing ourselves; believing that what we do in school is somehow not our real self, that we can split our being between 'teacher mode' and 'real person mode.' This dichotomy is unhelpful, and only serves to heighten our feelings of unease and isolation in our work.

Instead, we must be prepared to acknowledge that *how we react in school is as a result of everything that has gone on before in our lives* - that 'baggage' I referred to earlier. We can either choose to ignore this fact, or we can start to find ways of understanding things about our past experiences that can result in us feeling annoyed, confused, vulnerable or personally challenged by the behaviour of our pupils.

So why, for example, do I want to explode at that idle Year 7, Jake, who seems to think that late homework is the norm? It could be that I have a real concern for his well-being, and would hate to see his life choices whittled down by such an attitude. But it could also be for some of the reasons I've jotted down on the next page.

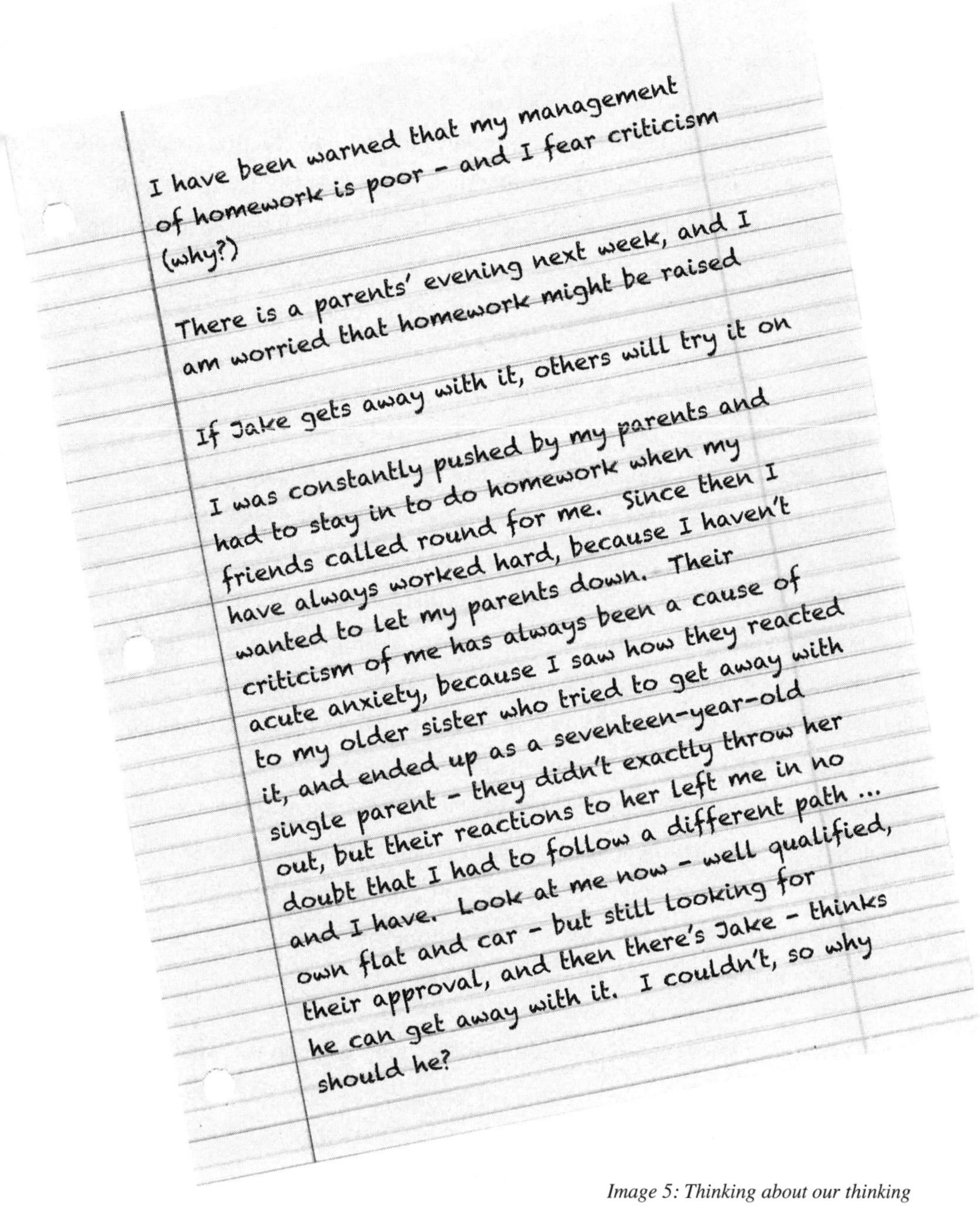

I have been warned that my management of homework is poor – and I fear criticism (why?)

There is a parents' evening next week, and I am worried that homework might be raised

If Jake gets away with it, others will try it on

I was constantly pushed by my parents and had to stay in to do homework when my friends called round for me. Since then I have always worked hard, because I haven't wanted to let my parents down. Their criticism of me has always been a cause of acute anxiety, because I saw how they reacted to my older sister who tried to get away with it, and ended up as a seventeen-year-old single parent – they didn't exactly throw her out, but their reactions to her left me in no doubt that I had to follow a different path ... and I have. Look at me now – well qualified, own flat and car – but still looking for their approval, and then there's Jake – thinks he can get away with it. I couldn't, so why should he?

Image 5: Thinking about our thinking

SCHOOL AS A SECURE BASE

Not every incident of late homework is likely to spark such an analytical thread (fortunately!). But each of us carries our own burdens and baggage from the past: seeing how these influence our present mindset and reaction to situations is the first real step to managing our thoughts. As Louise Bombèr points out (in Bombèr & Hughes, 2013), self-awareness is the first step towards self-control. And if we can manage our reactions and our thoughts, we really are in a strong position to -

- ✓ Understand what upsets, infuriates, inspires and elates us.
- ✓ Understand why colleagues might react to us in the way they do.
- ✓ Understand why pupils might react to us in the way they do.
- ✓ Understand just what is in our power to change - and what isn't.

The following is an approach into an area that could change your whole life, never mind what goes on in your classroom. Although it is straightforward in that it can be started immediately, without making appointments, or buying books or CDs, it does ask of you that you spend time on it, and that you are prepared to think deeply about what the influences are from your past that result in your present reactions to situations. I believe that if you are prepared to follow this approach, you will be able to come to an understanding as to why you act in the way you do, and how you can therefore change any 'knee jerk' reactions you find yourself having for those that are more positive and grounded in peace. The following few questions are a starting point.

- What do I know about my own thoughts/feelings/actions - what makes me tick?
- Am I a 'glass half full' or a 'glass half empty' person?
- Do I blame myself or others if things go wrong?

- Am I able to look in a mirror and say three positive things about myself?
- Can I accept praise graciously, or do I shrug it off with a self-deprecating comment?

Basically, the process I'm suggesting we start with is to develop our understanding of what motivates us *to do what we do, why we do it,* and what underpins *how we think about* what happens both in the world around us, and inside ourselves. This is also a classroom technique that has been successfully used to help children and young people come to an understanding of how thinking about their own thinking can be helpful at a number of very practical levels (*see* Appendix One p.189, *Metacognition*).

You may be the sort of person who is happy to start this type of reflective work on your own - if so, that's fine, and you can skip the next section, and begin with *'Write it all down!'* on p.41. But equally you may find it easier to talk such things through with someone else, in which case the next section, on peer mentoring, would be your starting point.

The reality for most of us, though, is perhaps a mixture of the two, and one approach may well lead to the other - and back again. Work out what works for you.

Peer mentoring: starting to talk about thoughts and feelings with someone else

The use of what has come to be described as 'peer mentoring' may be a way forward here. Peer mentoring involves finding another person with whom you can talk openly, and as such is really an extension of the wisdom embodied in the saying *"Come on - get it off your chest and you'll feel better!"*. The difference between just letting it all out and peer mentoring is that with the latter, we have a consistent and prepared listener, someone who has been chosen by us as a confidante, and who is aware of their role primarily as a listener, not as an all-knowing problem-solver. The aim of peer mentoring is to share our concerns in a safe, holding environment, and yes, somewhere we can shout, cry and rant if we need to, but always with the understanding that we are not being judged for how we think and feel, and that we are accepted for who we are.

The key to making the most of peer mentoring is to choose the right, trusted person to listen and question sympathetically, who is not an instructor or 'expert'. You might find a colleague in your own school, or a friend from your wider life, to be suitable. It could be a 'best friend', but it's essential that you can work together in total honesty and trust, rather than your peer mentoring partner thinking that they have to say what they think you want to hear in order to preserve your relationship. Equally, what passes between you has to be in confidence - there is no place for gossip between you or a third party about what either of you have discussed with your peer mentoring partner. Although not essential, it can be helpful if you are sharing in this process, both using the time to explore areas of concern and frustration, as well as joy and triumph, mutually supporting each other.

In this process of support and encouragement, keep the following in mind:

- ✓ The focus is on self-discovery.
- ✓ The partnership is genuine, and non-hierarchical.
- ✓ The process relies more on questions rather than instructions and immediate 'advice'.
- ✓ The overall tone of your sessions together is non-threatening and non-judgmental.
- ✓ The principles embodied in Solution Focussed Brief Therapy (SFBT) are of relevance here. SFBT originated in the 1960s as a result of a project on the West Coast of the USA to look at more effective ways of communication with individuals with a diagnosis

of schizophrenia. It ultimately depended on getting the client to stop doing what didn't work, and often making a 180 degree turn to look at the problem in another way. Rather than the listener and speaker talking round *the problem,* the focus shifts to *the person,* and how they might take small steps to resolve the issue. These small steps would be of the speaker's own making, rather than the listener coming up with solutions.

I became an unofficial mentor for a colleague in an English department who was a mature NQT. Dave was being driven to distraction by one particular Year 7 pupil, Liam, and asked if I would observe a lesson when he was teaching this boy's class. It was the last lesson of the day, and the class was clearly tired and a bit noisy. After Dave had settled them to work, I was able to observe the interactions between him and Liam - which were in many respects little different from his interactions with several other pupils.

After the lesson, and armed with a coffee, we sat down to chat, and I asked Dave to list all the things that really niggled him about Liam. We looked it over, and I then suggested that out of the seven points listed, Dave choose the three that he thought could be tackled next lesson. These became the focus for the rest of our chat, as to how he could react to, or plan to avoid, the issues from Liam that were annoying him. The three key issues were:

Poorly completed homework
Continually asking for help
Forever wanting to leave his place to sharpen his pencil, fetch another book, ask something of another pupil

Dave decided that he could take a bit more time to set homework and check that it was written in planners, that he could have a list of written instructions ready for Liam, and that possibly, with the security given by the instructions, there would be less need for the pupil to wander. None of these solutions were startling as such, but emerged from our chat and were made by Dave (I had suggested none of them directly), and left him feeling more in control of the situation. Dave went into his next lesson with the class feeling more confident, and although subject to the occasional blip, his relationship with Liam improved.

We were later able to spend another session chatting about this particular pupil and his wider background, and this further strengthened Dave's relationship with him.

Although school based, much of the above embodied the general principles of peer mentoring, as I was 'unofficial' in this support role, and chosen by Dave because of our general rapport.

Most sessions of peer mentoring will be out of school, and so it's important to commit to a regular pattern of meeting that is realistic, and not always open to cancellations. The location has to be one that is both relaxing but not noisy with other distractions. I've found that there is considerable virtue in 'walking and talking' - given weather that isn't too turbulent! If you decide on a domestic setting, try to pick a place and time that won't be compromised by children, partners or even demanding pets!

Once you start reflecting on your thinking, you might feel that counselling or spiritual support would be another way forward for you, but this takes us into a different sphere which might also have financial implications. My aim here is to encourage you to start talking with someone you trust, in a way that is simply at one remove from negative thinking, offers perspective, and which places you in the centre of a process that can help you -

▶   to understand something of the reasons why you react in the way
     you do,

and

▶   to explore how you *could* respond in ways that are more considered,
     relaxed, and ultimately of positive benefit to your own well-being.

At a recent workshop, a group of teachers listed the following qualities and abilities as being desirable in a peer mentor, and these form an excellent summary to this section:

⋆ Acceptance
⋆ Empathy
⋆ Understanding
⋆ Shared language
⋆ Containment
⋆ Allows space between thoughts and comments
⋆ Listens actively

Write it all down!

I suggested earlier (p.37) that you might be happier working on your own, in which case you might be starting the process of reflecting on your thinking here. It is equally valid though to combine elements of this section with peer mentoring, perhaps using some of the ideas that come to you between regular sessions as a jumping-off point for your next meeting.

MAKING LISTS

The advantage of a list is that it can be short! Following on from the lesson I observed above (on p.39), Dave scribbled down his seven niggles in a couple of minutes. A list isn't the place for deep analysis, but is a starting point. As well as listing the incidents in your day that left you feeling stressed, you could equally jot down the steps that have brought you to this stage in your life. For example:

- ☆ The people who have influenced me the most
- ☆ The people who I have liked/disliked the most
- ☆ What I wish I'd done differently in the past
- ☆ What I'm glad I did in the past
- ☆ What I like most/least about myself
- ☆ What I like most/least about my current school/head/colleagues
- ☆ The features I most like/dislike in my pupils
- ☆ What I would save from my home in a fire
- ☆ My past successes/failures
- ☆ My worst fears
- ☆ My greatest hopes

If you are a visual person, this could be extended by tearing images from magazines that represent elements from the lists, drawing, painting, sculpting … it really doesn't matter how you do this, but it is important that you make a start on a path that, in its next stage, will become more reflective. Keep the lists safe, whether you're using a note book or computer file. I'll give a few ideas as to how you can use these lists after the next section, *'Keep a log'*.

KEEP A LOG

Whether you're 'going it alone' or combining this with peer mentoring, keeping a diary/journal/audio log is a helpful way to deepen your thinking about your reactions to a situation or person. What you record here will be more reflective, based perhaps on a particular lesson, a whole day, a meeting, a peer mentoring session - it's up to you, but to be as inclusive as possible, aim for variety, not only highs or lows! You could include:

⋆ The good points in any school day, in order, as they come

⋆ Ditto the bad points!

⋆ A good/bad lesson, in any order - just record as the memories come to you

⋆ A 'micro-managed' lesson in great detail, from the first minute to … the tenth? The last bell?

Friday January 11th

Well that lesson left something to be desired! It's always the same - a bit of snow and the kids lose it. So does the heating system - you'd think reliable boilers would be a feature of the 21st century! Very helpful to be told that I could go to another room, when I'd got everything prepared in my own icebox. Wasn't ready for all the fuss about not being allowed to keep their top coats on though - but they know the rules as well as I do, and with GA in the next room I wasn't going to risk another bollocking. It was cold though, and then they started to moan about not being let out early and it would be my fault if they got stuck in the snow. That's when I lost it - they have no idea what it's like to drive 20 miles on ungritted roads. Last time anything like this happened I didn't get home until turned eight!

SCHOOL AS A SECURE BASE

GA's critical face at the door - Everything all right in here? - and Sharon would have slipped her coat back on, for him to haul her out into his room. That'll be a mention in dispatches at the Monday morning briefing ...

It is this log, together with the earlier lists, that will start to form the basis for the last section of this process.

Lists and Logs: great stuff, but how do they help us further on the way to a self-reflective process that ultimately will see us more peacefully orientated towards both ourselves and others? As stand-alones they have limited value, dealing as they do with the 'whats', with the straight descriptions of the things and events that we experience. So now we have to turn these into the basis for questions such as: *"Why do I list* these *particular people, why do I describe* these *events in* this *particular way?"* In other words, we need to start taking responsibility for the way we think, and the way we react, and if we want to change these reactions to ones that are calmer, less fraught and more peaceful, we need to understand what our habitual responses have become, and why.

TAKING PERSONAL RESPONSIBILITY
It is not enough for us to have a vague idea in our heads as to what we are finding out about our own thought processes, because past habitual thought patterns are very powerful, and will quickly overwhelm our new thoughts. We might hope to do things better next time, but the forces that have formed each of us are tenacious, and for a variety of reasons (including patterns of reaction that have to do more with our long distant ancestral survival than 21st century needs), they won't let go easily unless you and I are determined to move on. That is why we need to write things down, or verbalise our thoughts to another person, in order to start a process in which we can more accurately come to

understand why we have reacted in the way we have.

Let's turn again to that last lesson on Friday January 11th. How can it be used as the basis of genuine self-reflection that might leave our snow-bound colleague feeling more robust and calm in the face of what will be an inevitable Monday morning rap over the knuckles?

OK then - so why didn't I take up the offer to move rooms? At least I'd have been away from GA! I suppose I do value the security of my own space - I like the order of it all. Why? Always have I suppose ... think back - that room I shared when I was - how old? Six or seven? Real mess - couldn't stand it then, don't much like mess now.

Still today's change wouldn't have been forever - and wouldn't have had all that coat fuss. I guess if I'd have let them keep them on, they wouldn't have got so twitchy, I wouldn't have yelled, and Sharon wouldn't have dropped me in it. It wouldn't have been the end of the world if they had kept their coats on, and let's face it, hardly sets a precedent, not in these temperatures. And that's the thing - just thought back to that time when mum made us walk to school when the snow came up over my wellies. Couldn't miss school, oh no! A bit different nowadays with all the H&S concerns about enough staff being in, kids slipping and their parents wanting to sue the school. Daft! But why do I need things to be in such order, why can't I remember it's OK to have some flexibility? Difficult one - must mention it to Donna when we next get together.

No one entry in a reflective log is going to answer all the questions, but perhaps our colleague is on the way to finding out why some of the trigger points are what they are for him.

So when we're thinking about our pupils' behaviour, a really good starting point could be to question our own habitual responses when what pupils do is bewildering or challenging for us, bearing in mind that we are not going to change in days our responses which have taken years to establish.

Because ultimately the only person who can control me is myself - if that's what I want to do. Who do you want to control you? Others will always be lining up to take our place - to take control of us; people from the past, current friends, colleagues and others, and our own worries about the future. We can't always control what events come towards us, but we can increasingly control our reaction to them. Ultimately what we think, do and say does have a profound effect on all those around us, colleagues and pupils alike, and can also have a effect in determining what happens to us in the future. The 'self-fulfilling' prophecy has reality - as Henry Ford commented in the quote above (p.33).

So, throughout the process of coming to understand what makes you stressed and why, it's also equally important to tune your awareness to what makes you feel more positive - what makes you feel more energised and upbeat, because this will form the basis of placing your own well-being firmly in the centre of your concern.

Certain foods? Exercise? Being around certain people? A weekend away? Being creative? Celebrating success? Then don't be afraid to add these into the equation too. I am concerned that you do as much as you can to value and nurture your own well-being in all of this, and continue to do so long after finishing reading this book.

Starting a reflective process is not a 'quick fix', and in many ways is the foundation for much that follows. This doesn't mean that you have to have gone through lists and logs or peer mentoring to try any of the approaches that follow - in many cases, once again it's probably 'chicken and egg', and each can lead to the other. However, I do need to repeat that unless we are prepared to take on trying to find out how we feel and why we react to certain situations, the other techniques remain as 'bolt ons'. They may have a novelty factor at first, but if our old habitual reactions remain unchallenged, the effectiveness of the new will diminish as the old patterns and habits reassert themselves.

All of what I have been suggesting lies within our power. We can initiate all of it, maintain it and benefit enormously from it. It's free, private, and can be done anywhere, anytime. It can be done without financial outlay, but what is being asked for is time - time to meet, to talk, to write and to reflect. However, please rest assured that it will be time well spent, as it will start to place you back in the centre of your working life as a teacher, able to control what you can, and to understand that when situations are genuinely out of your hands, it is best not to fret, to resist, and to become impossibly frustrated by it all. Let's move away from seeing ourselves as people who have no choice but to suffer in such situations, toward a place where our ability to recover our peace of mind is fundamental.

At this point I would like to move away for a few moments from what we can do as individuals, and to share a whole school model that can be used to help us become more reflective in our work, and so bring into our classrooms a calmer, more peaceful approach. Whilst new in many schools, it is already well established elsewhere in social care and counselling.

Professional support

In my experience, there can often be a somewhat sad divide between the world of social care and education, each convinced that the other could serve the needs of children and young people much better if only they would listen to the other. Teachers complain that they can never contact social workers as they are 'never there' and 'don't do anything when you do contact them'. Social workers complain that teachers don't understand the restraints that are placed on what they can do, and that their case loads are such that they can't be sitting in an office at the end of a phone.

However, I think that there really is one area in which social care does seem to have the advantage, and that is in regular supervision between the social worker and their line manager (this is also an integral and crucial element in the way in which professional counsellors and therapists work). Supervision is a regular, timetabled meeting during which all aspects of the social worker's caseload and their working life in general are discussed within parameters laid down very clearly in a supervision agreement, a document signed by both parties. It is not appraisal, assessment or inspection, but it represents an acknowledgement that in an area of high stress work, without such a 'safety valve', there is the very real danger that secondary PTSD (post-traumatic stress disorder) can creep up insidiously on the social worker. Similarly, the line manager is supervised and so on - and no, I'm not sure where this buck stops, unless the Director seeks peer mentoring with a colleague in another LA!

I have worked for a decade in a multi-disciplinary team of teachers and social workers, and have benefited greatly from this process. The arguments against applying the supervision model to schools is so often based on logistics, rather than anything deemed to be intrinsically wrong with the idea itself. However, research undertaken by Ann Beynon (2003) as part of an MSc project into the transfer of such a support model into education points to other possibilities: that, for example, in schools where the head teacher is in sympathy with such work, it is possible to establish a model of counselling supervision *that serves the needs of teachers*, giving them an opportunity for reflection and support.

Interestingly, teachers found the term 'supervision' unhelpful, perhaps hinting too much at a hierarchical relationship. Instead, the term 'professional support' was more resonant for them, but whatever the name given to the rose ...

The teachers taking part in Beynon's research identified the following needs that professional support would have to fulfil:

✓ To create a space secure enough to be open and honest.
✓ For the teacher to be able to talk about his or her experiences with pupils.
✓ For the teacher to be able to share his or her attitudes and classroom strategies.
✓ For supervision to take place within a work setting, thus avoiding the teacher taking the problem home with him or her.

There are considerable implications for enabling this kind of regular professional support to become embedded in a school. Such a process depends on a head teacher being suitably sympathetic. If you are fortunate enough to work in a school with such a head teacher, then this might suggest that some of the more acute problems and stresses faced by many teachers will be less prevalent, given that the SMT will already be looking sympathetically at ways in which the daily demands on staff can be lessened, and the well-being of all staff is recognised as paramount to the overall success of the school.

Nevertheless, the provision of professional support is a strongly validated model. As long ago as 1955, the need for teachers to 'face themselves' was identified by Jersild, and those processes we have just been looking at, whether as a result of school or individual initiative, can only enhance a peaceful school, and add credibility to the belief that *Every Teacher* (as well as Child) *Matters.*

As teachers we are natural communicators, though this communication tends to be from us to 'them' - pupils, parents, and colleagues. It is a two-way process of course - we need to listen to what is said to us. However, it is now time for us *to communicate with ourselves*, to listen to our drives, fears and motivations, and to understand that by achieving a deepening level of self-understanding we will be in a position to rise above the habitual reactions that only serve to produce 'more of the same' - when what we need is peace, calm and joy.

Talking, writing, reflective logs, professional support - all have a vital role to play in helping us come to a point when we can review and re-evaluate what we do and why we do it. A further element in this process is being able to quieten our restless, over-active brains, our frantic helter-skelter thoughts that push us first one way and then the other - whilst underneath the buzz and whirr are all those habits of thought and reaction that have become our 'default setting' when confronted by any new challenge or demand.

If we are to really think about our thinking, we must be able to slow down and stand aside from the whirling speed of daily life. We don't have to become the Dalai Lama or go on a retreat. But to slow down, we are going to need to still our minds. So this is where we go next …

HeartMath®

PROCESS STARTING

So - is this it?

This quiet sitting
My mind flitting
From the shopping
To the marking
And to tonight's draw
And just how I'd spend it -
With the dentist's appointment -
To be changed
Rearranged - damn!

Is this it?
Be still and breathe
In to five
Out to five
In to five

Now is the moment
Now is now
Now is ... Year 9's earlier today
Vile, rude, noisy
Little animals ...
Well, now is now
They are not here
They are not here
Now is -
Breathe in to five
Out to five
In to five
Out to - to -
Tired - eyes sleepy -

Sleep - sl ... ss ....

Without embarking too much on a Stream of Consciousness process, the problems and distractions involved when you first start to 'still the mind' are not unique or odd - everyone experiences them, but everyone who persists will tell you that the mind can be 'emptied', and into this still space peace can stream.

The techniques for achieving this stillness of mind all have certain features in common - selecting a quiet place, comfortable clothing, a supportive posture that is not too relaxing (wake up!), suitable lighting, perhaps a candle flame to focus on, and a quiet determination to return to a still mind when at the beginning our minds inevitably flit from one distraction to another.

As an alternative to straightforward breathing meditation, which may not be for everyone, I'll next describe a technique which I have personally experienced and seen work across the board, with pupils, as well as staff, parents, and stressed OFSTED inspectors amongst others ...

It is known by the name of HeartMath® and is a trusted and validated technique that is only now finding its way into schools from extensive use in industry and commerce. It uses the power of positive thinking and visualisation, as well as simple breathing techniques. The results of using HeartMath are simple but profound. In a relatively short period of time we can physiologically alter the way our heart influences our brain, and the subsequent release of positive 'feel good' hormones. High blood pressure, anxiety, sleeplessness - can all be managed in a positive and painless way. It is this that I am advocating on the road to creating peaceful schools; teachers who can pause, consider, evaluate and come to a balanced decision in the face of challenge from whatever quarter.

The analogy of the heart as a mechanical pump, and nothing more, had its origins in 18th century scientific discovery. Before that, our language was rich in connections made between the heart and emotions: broken-hearted, hard-hearted, warm-hearted - and of course, to all matters of love. But with the dawn of mechanisation and industrialisation, knowledge about these affective links was eroded, and as the heart kept loyally chugging away, we were led to believe that our emotional life might be simply to do with hormones, specific areas of the brain, or even evolutionary survival.

It is only in the last twenty years or so that neuroscience has discovered physiological and hormonal links between the heart and the brain, showing that our hearts are more than just pumps, and that a healthy emotional life is crucial to a healthy heart. More than this: over the last decade, research has homed in on the links between a 'relaxed' heart and the production of the hormone oxytocin, the so-called 'love hormone'.

One such conclusion, that links the very real physical impact of this relationship on our bodies comes from the *Brazilian Journal of Medical and Biological Research*:

> We have reasons to believe that local oxytocin production in the heart
> is physiologically relevant.   Gutkowska & McMann, 2000

The key to a calm, positive heart lies in what is called *heart rate variability* (HRV), and it is this that underpins whether our heart is functioning in a way that is called *coherent*. Coherence in this context means being consciously joyful and harmonious, both with ourselves and with others.

HRV is the pattern of heart activity that can be measured and shown in a wave pattern, and demonstrates whether we are stressed or peaceful. The vibrational energy it creates becomes our heart's electro-magnetic field, that radiates from the body for several feet, reacting with those other electromagnetic fields it comes into contact with. If our HRV is coherent, the effect on others is positive - and the converse is also true. *Coherence* in your heart rate variability will result in a feeling of easiness within me. A *lack of coherence* for you, on the other hand, will have the effect of unease on me.

Similarly, coherence in our heart rate variability can positively influence the efficient working of our own internal organs. The concept of 'cellular memory' is increasingly widely accepted, that is, that each cell in our body contains within it a mini-brain, and the more complex the organ, the more developed its 'brain' function. This complexity culminates with the heart; investigations carried out with heart transplant patients which validate this were first made widely known with the 1997 publication of Claire Sylvia's book *A Change Of Heart*. These investigations show that in a significant number of cases, the recipient of the new heart starts to exhibit the behavioural traits, preferences, and emotions of their heart's donor.

All of this has emphasised that the coherence and optimal functioning of the brain is dependent on the coherence of the heart. The more detailed and complex the research in this area, the more there emerges a pattern of human physiology that emphasises the complex, amazing interplay of our body's chemistry, and all hat makes us human.

Back in the 1970s, a group in California founded The HeartMath® Institute, aiming to find ways of bringing to the wider public the then ground-breaking research into these dynamic interrelationships between the heart, the brain and the release of positive hormones between a coherent heart and the brain. They found a very real link between controlled breathing, positive visualisation and coherence in HRV. Further to this, they developed a bio-feedback software program that showed in real time how controlled breathing could positively affect HRV.

The software has subsequently been modified for use with children as well as adults. Results are impressive. The training was first offered to multi-nationals to combat executive burn-out, and North Sea oil companies to reduce accident rates on oil rigs. Following on from the success of this training, its use has been gradually extended to many schools, residential homes, and Young Offender Institutes.

The use of the software has an undoubted 'wow factor' for both adults and children. The impact that having an ear or finger sensor connect you to a computer, that then shows you that by simple breathing you are able to bring your HRV into healthy coherence, is considerable. In Chapter 3, (*Bringing Peace to Pupils*), I will give more details as to how HeartMath® can be used with classes and individual pupils to bring about positive changes in behaviour and learning. For us though, the good news is that the principles behind HeartMath® are equally effective *without* the software investment (good as it is), and can be practised at any time during the day.

There are various levels of breathing and visualisations suggested by HeartMath® training, but in brief, the process is as shown on the opposite page.

Sit quietly in an upright chair.

Control your breathing in to the count of five, out to the count of five.

Visualise your breath coming in and out through your heart - if it helps, place your hand over your heart.

Once this pattern of breathing is established, have a picture in your mind of an event, person or situation that has given you pleasure.

Move on from that to getting in touch with the actual feelings that pleasure represents, and home in on these.

Continue this for about ten minutes.

You will gain the best results with four sessions a week - though there is nothing to stop you doing more.

Image 6: Steps to heart coherence

The great advantage of HeartMath® is that it can be practised at any time, to both relieve stress and bring about a release of the hormones that are responsible for feeling good. It is one of those techniques that can, by themselves, bring about considerable benefits without further incursions into self-examination.

Ironically, though, adopting its use is probably a strong indication that you are also willing to look at life through a different lens, and the relaxation it brings can help to release thought processes that reinforce metacognition (p.33). In other words, this is a process that can help you relax, clear your mind of the weight of habitual thoughts, and so pave the way to being able to examine what you do and why you do it. As a result, you will be able to move to a peaceful, relaxing and invigorating state of mind in preparation for your first lesson tomorrow.

Those of you who are familiar with meditative breathing will quickly conclude that the underlying principles of HeartMath® are thousands of years old, harking back to times when intuition was the guiding light in many areas that have since been overhauled by mechanistic science. Happily, we are now in a position to synthesise these streams, and to reap the rewards.

Finally, research carried out in 2006 by a HeartMath® training consultancy, Hunter Kane, with head teachers and staff across the country - the East Midlands, the North West and the Home Counties - recorded significant reductions in stress (characterised by tiredness and exhaustion, poor sleep, aches and pains, anxiety and depression). For staff, percentage drops were typically from 59% suffering from stress to 21% after HeartMath® intervention, and for headteachers these two figures were 64% and 13% respectively. Such findings serve to underline the effectiveness of this type of intervention in promoting more peaceful, less stressed teachers, and can certainly help us to understand why below, the appearance of Darren in surly teenage mode is dealt with rather more effectively ...

DOWN THE LINE

Now, how did that happen?
Again, it had to be Darren
Slinging late into class
Flinging coat and bag
To the back
Hunched defiance.

The shout came to my lips
But died again.
Darren's problems are not mine
I am fine
I am fine
I can quietly approach
And quietly speak:

"When you're settled ..."
"I'd like you to ..."
"Can you please ..."
"Could you just ..."

Darren glances up
Eyes me up
Drops his head
Mumbles
"Yeah, whatever - OK"

The class waits
I return
To the front
Smile
And continue

This moment passes into the next.

Have we got to half term yet?

With luck and perseverance, some of the processes outlined above are starting to become a reality for you. The eyeball-to-eyeball confrontation with Darren that might have been the past habitual reaction to that kind of behaviour has been replaced with a calmer, more grounded approach from the teacher, which may actually leave Darren relatively speechless. And Darren is at least still in class, more prepared to engage than if a shouting match with Sir/Miss had left him spiked on adrenaline and cortisol.

Nor is this new situation, this change of approach, a sign of acquiescence or a 'backing down' on the teacher's part. Out of the teacher's own peaceful base, he or she has become able to use elements of assertive discipline to engage Darren with a request to work, without pushing him into a humiliating corner (and thus the need to save face) in front of his mates.

It is worth noting down some of the key points that underline assertive discipline, but viewing them in the context of a teacher who is utilising them out of their own calm space:

- ✓ Be positive from the very first, and demonstrate the attitudes and responses you are looking for.
- ✓ Nowhere is this more marked than in the tone and register of voice you use - shout, and Darren will shout back!
- ✓ Smile when you welcome the class into your room.
- ✓ Move in to speak to a pupil, but be aware of your body language - most communication is non-verbal.
- ✓ Respect personal space, and if you need to stand close, try to avoid a stance that might be misunderstood as 'squaring up'
- ✓ Move away once you have spoken to Darren - hovering over him can be intimidating, and also gives him the message that you don't have confidence that he will engage. Moving away also gives him the chance to appear to engage of his own volition - face therefore saved!
- ✓ If Darren still fails to comply, use patient repetition, letting him see you jot his name down, giving him closed alternatives - all are ways that can still avoid bloody-minded confrontation.

At the end of all this, Darren might possibly still be hell-bent on confrontation and other school sanctions might have to be used; but these are now a matter of last resort, rather than a frantic knee-jerk response from a teacher who is also on the edge of panic and disintegration.

Using sensory space

Although for much of this chapter I have emphasised the fact that bringing peace into our own classrooms and schools can be achieved by our own endeavour and initiatives, the earlier section on 'Professional Support' pre-supposed the willingness of a head teacher to initiate a whole school policy. The description of the work of 'A Quiet Place Ltd', makes a similar assumption. The following description of 'A Quiet Place' initially focussed on the needs of children, but I have included it here since schools which participated in the project soon found that staff (and later parents) were also able to benefit from the practices that make the project so successful.

'A Quiet Place' was established in the late 1990s by Penny Moon (www. aquietplace.co.uk). Its whole ethos could lie at the heart of a secure and peaceful school, but it depends on the close support of a head teacher for it to become embedded within the school's culture. And this time, 'embedded' is a physical reality, as the work is based on a specific physical space within a school.

A room is designed and decorated to enhance relaxation, and is intended to look as little like a classroom as possible. Sound, light, colour, and a number of specific interventions (over the years these have included aromatherapy, reflexology, psychotherapy, storytelling, and HeartMath®) are used to benefit children who are on the verge of exclusion. Children can self-refer to a six week programme which is monitored closely, and results have been consistently impressive. These are detailed in research undertaken by The University of Liverpool in *Inclusive Education Review* (Winter 2002/3).

The benefit for teachers in these schools, and why I'm including 'a Quiet Place' in this section, is two-fold. Children with difficult behaviours are speedily calmed and re-engaged, making the whole classroom environment calmer and more positive. But staff are also encouraged to make use of the room and these techniques at the end of the school day for themselves. Schools where teachers were on the verge of leaving have seen higher staff retention and lower turnover rates (*British Journal of Special Education*, September 2000).

Keeping the ball rolling - persistence

So let's imagine you make a start with some of the things I've been suggesting, and you notice some benefit. How can any of us make sure that we keep going with changes like this, and keep learning from them? The whole process of looking at ourselves and opening up the possibility of changing our viewpoint is one which requires us to develop persistence. To begin with, a thousand distractions will push their way in, and old thought habits die hard! The images opposite chart this process and may help to encourage us if we are derailed in our early attempts.

Whether we are able to access support through our own schools as a result of management-led initiatives, or whether we decide to 'go it alone', the learning cycle involved in making a change will be the same. We will move from *contemplation* (in this case, contemplation of why we react in the way we do, with the ultimate goal of allowing peacefulness to become the foundation of our future reactions): to *action* (making choices and changes): to *maintenance*: to *further contemplation* at what is now a deeper level of reflection. And so the cycle continues.

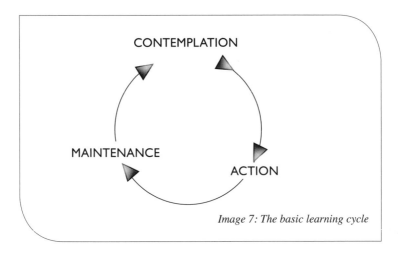

Image 7: The basic learning cycle

If this third element, *maintenance*, which signifies successful change, fails, the alternative is *relapse*, resulting in a return to stress states, when we stop practising or when we get frustrated with our own slow progress.

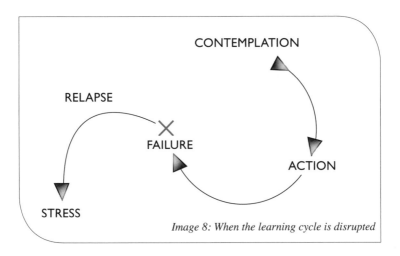

Image 8: When the learning cycle is disrupted

However, if we can learn from our failure through further *contemplation* and attempting to understand (rather than abandoning our new initiative) there may be a further revolution of the cycle, hopefully finding new elements of peacefulness. If we can learn from failure, our new habits will be maintained.

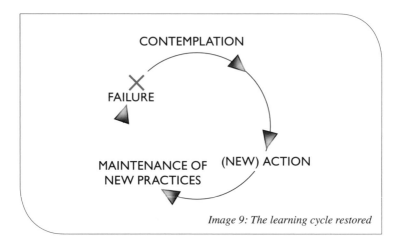

Image 9: The learning cycle restored

When we are contemplating why our new ways of responding are not making the difference we'd hoped for, our use of a 'peer mentor' has an invaluable role to play. Learning from mistakes and persistent practice will, over time, enable each of us to be better able to cope with changes of policy and curriculum that are totally beyond our control. Teachers will be better able to engage positively with children and young people who desperately need adults in their lives who are emotionally mature and able to model positive behaviour and attitudes. Everybody wins, when we as teachers prioritise our own inner state of peacefulness, and spend time on developing our own well-being.

Humour

There is a final element to consider here, and that's humour. Of course when we're extremely stressed, laughter and humour are the last things we may feel like - *"Don't make me laugh! What have we got to laugh about?"*

For many years, *The Readers Digest* regularly ran a feature *Laughter: the best medicine.* More recent medical research has validated the incredibly positive healing that can take place as a result of regular laughter. Jo Brighouse, a Midlands primary school teacher, took up this theme when she wrote:

> Educational theorists and psychologists have done plenty of research into the link between humour and learning. You can't move in a Waterstone's education section for books highlighting the proven link between laughter and learning … if you are relaxed and having fun you are more likely to pick stuff up. Surely this is no different for teachers? Teachers laden down with paperwork and with their head's menacing demand to 'get levels up or else' ringing in their ears are unlikely to be entering the classroom with a spring in their step.
>
> *TES*, 13.7.12

Even though it is unlikely that we will be seeing INSET on humour in the near future, we can hope that teachers who are suitably peaceful will be able to see the funny side of things when appropriate, and will be able to bring this lightness of touch into their own teaching. My sense is that with peacefulness comes the ability to take life more lightly.

We all know we laugh more when we're happy, when we're enjoying ourselves. Peacefulness is a way to bring that enjoyment and that lightness back into our teaching, when we can welcome our pupils each day with a genuine smile of warmth and recognition, and when we can laugh sympathetically at the mistakes we will all make from day to day.

END OF TERM

I stand by the door
As they shamble out
Shuffle to a halt
Each in front of me.

Half smiles
An embarrassed smirk
The Gangsta grips my hand
Grins and is gone.

My heartfelt wishes
To each of them
For a good break
Linger in the empty room.

An odd ball of paper
Not much, is binned
Desks, past their best
But graffiti free.

Silence, stillness.
God, I'm tired,
But actually - I'm OK
Water the plants
Then I'm away.
OK
OK
Yeah - OK

Phew - made it to the end of term! But just 'to make it' isn't really good enough, and speaks of desperate fatigue, numbed emotions and a craving for a holiday that will fail to deliver as so much expectation is heaped on its shoulders. Even the heady six week summer break can see a tripartite division of two weeks recovery, two weeks away and two weeks getting wound back up to a state of stress that started the tension ball rolling in the first instance. I've lost count of the number of teachers I've worked with over the last ten years in an organisation that offers fewer holidays, but with a very differently managed stress quotient, who are amazed that they don't actually miss the long school holidays they used to crave in their previous posts.

No-one in their right mind will maintain that teaching isn't tiring. In the best-run school in the land, the constant daily dynamic play between one adult and up to a hundred and thirty teenagers (or one adult and up to thirty lively children in constant contact) demands energy levels and alertness that cannot be appreciated by anyone who has never experienced such work. And no - it hasn't always been like this.

Historically, the master sitting at his desk, calmly marking books whilst his class studiously worked their way, in silence, through that day's exercise, was a reality, and one which has been carried in society's collective memory of the nine to four 'cushy' job. However, times have changed, the goal posts have been moved so many times that they keep falling over, and teachers are expected to be the all-singing/all-dancing/outcome-delivering/society-scape-goating/innovating/ behaviour-modifying supermen and women who would not have been recognised fifty years ago.

For us teachers, there is no going back to some 'golden age'. For if the well-ordered grammar school was at one end of the spectrum, the inner city sink 'sec mod' was at the other, but one that could see order maintained with cane, slipper, board rubber (thrown) or whatever implement fell immediately into the hand of the ex-serviceman whose most immediate life-experiences were brutal and bloody.

And now, as these former models slip and slide into the past, we have an educational system of which so much is expected by all sectors of society.

SCHOOL AS A SECURE BASE

Expectations have evolved a thousand-fold, and continue to do so at a pace that is hectic and incredibly demanding. There is little sign of this slowing up. And those at the centre of it all, the class and subject teachers, the TAs, the heads of year, the lunch time supervisors, the managers and SMT, all have to find coping mechanisms.

This is why I believe that at the heart of every successful school, one that wants to enhance the life chances of all its pupils and all its students by creating a safe and secure base for them, at the school's heart is the teacher who is aware of what can be done, and what can't, who is aware of his or her own needs, and who is prepared to stop and examine just what it is that makes them tick before they attempt to alter the lives of those they teach.

There is mounting evidence from all quarters that positive visualisation, mindfulness, supportive relationships, stress-busting sports and mind-calming meditation all combine to improve physical health and enhance the whole experience of being alive, no matter what your age or role in life. That this has to be true for teachers should be emblazoned in letters six foot high!

To switch from images of a comprehensive school to thinking about a concentration camp is a huge mental leap, but I would like to end this chapter with the wisdom that emerged from Auschwitz in the work of Viktor Frankl, who after 1945 became Professor of Neurology and Psychiatry at the University of Vienna's Medical School.

Frankl survived three years of incarceration in the death camps of World War II, and during this time was able to both survive as an integrated person himself, and to observe survival strategies in others. In his book *Man's Search for Meaning* (1959) he shares his deepest belief as to what contributed to his survival:

> Between stimulus and response, there is space. In that space lies our freedom to choose our response. In our response lies our growth and our happiness.

For Viktor Frankl this meant a daily, almost hourly, reassessment of all that he had thought and believed prior to his arrest, as he attempted to grapple, and come to terms with, examples of some of the worst obscenities one human being could inflict on another.

For us, the stakes can never be as high or as extreme. But out of the cauldron that Frankl experienced comes advice to us all, advice that points us in the direction of making choices based on authentic reasons, reasons that have been refined by our own attempts to look deep into ourselves as we follow the quest to find calmness and peacefulness in the way we work as teachers.

Section one

In summary

★ You are the most important force for change in your working life. Whatever external factors weigh down on you, you can modify their effects by changing your reaction to them, whether they are the latest government 'brainwave', or a turbulent teen during your last lesson of a long week.

★ As a result of considering and practising these techniques, you will be in a position to gain control of your reactions, and so, out of a sense of inner peace and calm, extend this to your whole teaching environment.

THESE TECHNIQUES INCLUDE:

→ Metacognition: stopping to think about why you think and react in the way you do.

→ Peer mentoring: working with a trusted friend to explore issues around your working life.

→ Writing it all down: reading back what you've put down can help clarify your thinking.

→ Supervision/Professional support: where possible, and with the support of a sympathetic head, finding ways to bring this into your school.

→ HeartMath®: one of the many techniques used to promote reflective relaxation, but one that has been soundly researched and proven.

→ Using sensory space: an example of what can be achieved given a whole school approach

→ Persistence: realising there are ways around setbacks

→ Humour: the lightness this can bring to our classrooms, and to ourselves.

★ We all need to remind ourselves and each other that teachers are the most important elements of our schools. If we are stressed, agitated, depressed and disengaged, our pupils will rapidly mirror this back to us. If we only 'muddle through', so will they.

★ But if we are able to develop the inner resources that are actually available to each one of us, we - and our pupils - will shine!

Section two

BRINGING PEACE TO PUPILS

If your plan is for one year, plant rice.

If your plan is for ten years, plant trees.

If your plan is for one hundred years, educate children.

Confucius

The class is working well, and I move round to each pupil advising, encouraging, and occasionally reminding an individual to return to the task in hand. I am met by smiles, and questions that show me how much is being understood.

At times a pupil is felt moved to help another, either with a difficult concept or in a more practical way. One group are clearly in control of the subject matter, and I take them to one side and ask them to research another aspect of the topic, with the aim of them presenting this at the start of the next lesson. They readily agree, and a couple leave the room to go to the resource centre for further information.

Suddenly a pupil who is very new to the class pushes their desk away and starts to cry. I move to her side, and, mindful of what I have been told of her challenging background, I start to talk quietly with her, using the techniques from last week's course on working with such behaviours. I ask the distressed pupil if she can help me with a job I need to complete in sorting out some art material for the next lesson, and after ten minutes she is clearly calmer.

I glance up at the clock and realise it will soon be time to start to wind up and ...

THE BELL!! What? Alarm ... Oh grief! Morning already - Monday morning and so that means ... Nooooooo! Just another ten minutes ...

But that dream - huh! Dream on ...

Does such a scenario have to remain in cloud cuckoo land, though? I would like to think that once we have examined our own responses to classroom challenge and stress as outlined in Section One, we will be in a strong position to look at the other side of the equation, the pupil. I'll be looking at the following elements in turn:

- ✓ The teacher can bring peace to the pupil by how she responds from the moment the pupil enters the classroom.
- ✓ The teacher can bring peace to the pupil by being flexible enough to suggest an alternative individual activity that more sensitively meets a sudden need.
- ✓ The teacher can bring peace to the pupil by having confidence in her own ability to respond from an attitude that is not immediately judgmental.

Teachers can bring peace to pupils through our own state of peacefulness

As I mentioned in the Introduction, over the last few years, there have been many initiatives which have attempted to embed 'peace' in our schools (*see* p.6). All these are very valuable and necessary to redress the balance from past practices. However, they could be seen as 'bolt on' additions. Such strategies are likely to remain on the surface unless they are embedded within teachers who are able to respond out of their own deeply embodied and peaceful sense of well-being. As well meant as these initiatives are, they will not bring peace or security into the core of pupil's lives and will slide away at some point in the future when the staff who promote them are no longer on the scene.

At this point I'd like to take a step back for a moment to look at the whole context, to see what might need to be in place before we can expect stand-alone peace-oriented interventions to truly become embedded. For many children a path to peacefulness will be one they can accept and build on; but the whole concept of 'peace' is alien to a significant minority, because their lives to date have been anything but peaceful and secure. So in this section I will be examining just what it is in the early years of some of our pupils that could have left them exposed, vulnerable and little able to consider 'peace' as a way of approaching school, other pupils or even themselves. This is necessarily going to involve us looking at certain aspects of child development.

Without a secure understanding as to what motivates, drives and inhibits children's learning as they develop, our teaching is going to involve a lot of wasted effort and misdirected good intentions. It might be supposed that ITT (Initial Teacher Training) and subsequent CPD (Continuing Professional Development) would cover this aspect of teaching, but little time is spent on these aspects of child development, and vital items in a teacher's tool kit are left unused or even left out of the original packing (*this is explored in more detail*

SCHOOL AS A SECURE BASE

on p.111 'Who will Train the Trainers?')

Back in 1948 the Morris Minor was launched to universal critical acclaim. Although there is a certain trend for some car manufacturers today to produce new models incorporating retro design features, the technology under the skin of cars rolling off the production line is bang up to date. However, in the world of education, many practices and assumptions replicate what might have been acceptable 50 years ago, but which simply haven't kept pace with everything that is now known regarding brain development and the conditions that best facilitate real learning. We are still driving round in Morris Minors largely oblivious of what is in today's showrooms. So I'll be helping you to trade in that old Morris for the latest green, energy saving hybrid.

Once we understand where our pupils have become 'stuck' in a place of no peace, because of their early backgrounds, we will be able to meet their needs, and in bringing peace and calm into their learning, spread it throughout our classrooms and schools.

Hopefully Section One will have persuaded you that the best person - indeed the only person - who can truly calm you is you yourself. We looked at a number of techniques to bring ourselves into a peaceful place, all of which have a proven success rate. We now know it is possible to stand back from habitual reactions to stressful situations in order to find a response that is going to bolster our own well-being and lead to a more successful outcome. If we can see how this works for ourselves we can now move on to consider just how such an outlook can positively impact on our pupils.

From p.94, I'll be introducing three specific techniques that have been proven to be effective in helping pupils discover peaceful ways of thinking, feeling, moving and working that will leave them feeling safe, secure and held.

The following case study might seem extreme, but is not uncommon - and the ripple effect of one 'Katie' in a class can be highly disruptive.

Eight year old Katie had experienced more trauma in her short life than most of us, thankfully, will experience in a life time. Sexually abused, a witness to appalling domestic violence, and then having to cope with the suspicious death of her mother, Katie was now in care, and not coping at school.

It was my role to support her in school, and to try to avoid what was seen as an inevitable permanent exclusion. Katie was restless in class, verbally abusive to most teachers (but sweetly compliant with the headteacher), physically abusive to other pupils, and would run out of class if challenged about her behaviour. Prior to coming into care, Katie had missed a lot of school, as she stayed at home to 'look after' her mother. Although weak in many areas of literacy and especially numeracy, she was unwilling to accept help in class, and became agitated if the teacher appeared to 'know' more than she did. At home Katie would soil herself and smear, but at school this seemed to be limited to occasionally wetting herself. Needless to say, other pupils avoided her, and Katie frequently found herself isolated at playtime, either through 'choice', or because of behaviour towards other pupils that led to her being taken back into class.

Katie's class teacher was at a loss as to how to regulate her behaviour, and Katie was succeeding in projecting her anxieties, fears and uncertainties onto her teacher. Daily challenge, conflict and final removal from class to the head's office was becoming the norm.

I suggested that we found time to meet on a weekly basis - the head, class teacher, SENCO, and myself to share what we were experiencing, and to crosscheck that everything that Katie was claiming to have happened to her was consistent and true. This had an immediate beneficial effect for the class teacher, who no longer felt isolated and disempowered. I was able to feed into this how Katie had been at home, and how the way Katie was presenting was no more the school's fault than Katie's.

I shared a number of strategies that I was able to implement myself during the four sessions I spent in school each week. These included creating a 'secure' work station for Katie at her own desk, and instant access to paper and crayons to 'doodle' in ways that were underpinned by Brain Gym (see p.94 below). At one point when she had run out of class I found Katie starting to dress up with play clothes that had been brought in for the infants. This led to many sessions in which I would take Katie out of class to play shop. She would dress up as different customers, and using play money and pretend goods from the infants we would start to count and so on - Katie was the customer and able to control the situation. We would end these sessions by going outside to play ball, catching, and French cricket.

Is there a happy ending? Within school, Katie's behaviour started to improve, and her anxiety levels visibly decreased - as did those of her class teacher. At the end of the summer term, Katie was allowed to go and live with a family member. Within four weeks the placement had broken down, and after two emergency short term placements Katie was a placed at a residential therapeutic home in the south west.

My interventions with Katie were based very much on what I had come to learn about child development, and the development of the brain. Using this knowledge can impact very positively on how we come to react to children who are clearly anxious and stressed, and unable to learn because of this. I believe that if we are going to create the right peaceful environment that will help to optimise our pupils' learning and development, bringing together what is scientifically proven about child development with our own calm, mindful teaching is essential.

So from this section, you will ...

✓ Understand what has been discovered regarding brain development, secure attachment and learning.

✓ Realise why more space needs to be given to pupils experiencing trauma.

✓ Look at the difference between ADHD and Attachment Difficulties (AD).

✓ Pick up tips from the world of Brain Gym and HeartMath®.

✓ Come to appreciate and respect the complex interplay between brain, heart and emotions in the process of learning.

✓ Have an introduction to an exciting, innovative and simple programme that is bringing peace to pupils and students around the world.

From before the cradle ...

We know that many behaviours derive their origins from what happens in a child's earliest years, but understanding how this process starts from even before birth is vital to helping us think about and meet the needs of the children in our classes.

It's increasingly recognised that the emotional and physical well-being of an expectant mother is crucial to the well-being of her unborn child. The effects of smoking, drug and alcohol abuse on foetal development are well-documented. For instance, one 2008 American study estimated that up to 30% of teenage pregnant mothers took illicit drugs. The impact of this abuse on the foetus can extend from the stunting of physical limbs to the underdevelopment of internal organs. If unchecked, such abuse can result in premature birth, underweight babies and in some cases infants with substance dependency inherited from the womb.

Such levels of stress impact negatively on the physical well-being of babies and young children. In particular, continual, unmodified stress triggers the release of the hormone cortisol. In small amounts cortisol is necessary, but in the unregulated flood brought on by stress, it is toxic. Left unchecked it will:

- Bring on digestive disorders.
- Bring on aches and pains in joints.
- Increase blood pressure and cardio vascular disease.
- Limit the absorption of calcium, compromising bone structure (see for instance articles in *The Lancet,* 2:597, 1979, and *The American Journal of Physiology,* 257, 1989. In other words, this information has been available for some time!).
- Limit any higher level thinking skills by bringing the body into a flight/fight mode.
- Potentially contribute to depression and bipolar disorder.

As a result of the work done through the Avon Longitudinal Survey of Parents and Children which was started in 1991/2, we know what some of the long term effects of increased cortisol are. This study has tracked 14,000 mothers and their children, and in 2005 research based on this by Dr Thomas O'Connor reported as follows:

> We found that anxiety in late pregnancy was associated with higher levels of cortisol in children many years later. Elevated levels of cortisol are associated with psychological risk or psychological disturbance, notably depression and anxiety.
>
> *Biological Psychiatry*, 2005

To understand why compromise of this type in the developing brain of the foetus has such a negative impact on some of our pupils in their struggle to find any kind of peace, we need to take a quick look even further back, at how we have survived so far as a species.

At a simple structural level, the brain has three parts. Firstly, the brain stem/reptilian brain, which deals with basic survival techniques: secondly, the middle/limbic brain, which deals with emotional responses; and finally, the higher brain, the neo-cortex, which processes those thinking functions that make us uniquely human. Over the millennia these three have unfolded, but the basic default setting in times of danger has been the first of these three, the one that kicks in when a threat is perceived.

"I didn't think - I just hit him!" "Get your hands off me or I'll kill you!" The kind of comment we so often hear when sorting out a flare up of tempers in the classroom or playground is largely true, because when the reptilian brain takes charge, higher thinking is effectively blocked until the danger is past. That's fine when confronted with a very hungry sabre-toothed tiger. That's not the time to admire the markings on its fur, or inwardly debate latest research into its development as a predator. It's time to scarper, aided by a burst of adrenaline, or to hurl your spear with superhuman strength. The third F from the three primitive reactions of fight, flight - freeze - might not be the best idea either ... as you may

end up as breakfast, your genes removed from the human evolutionary pool.

Unfortunately, aspects of our socialisation and development as higher thinking individuals haven't brought the necessary change in our instinctive default setting: so something perceived as a threat, whilst no longer necessarily life-threatening, can still trigger an unthinking, violent response. Within our classroom, a perceived threat directed at a vulnerable youngster can trigger a totally disproportionate response from them, resulting in chaos and confusion.

So let's go back to the newly born baby, whose mother has been subject to stress and emotional anguish during her pregnancy, never mind any direct substance abuse. Her levels of adrenaline have been constantly on overload, and this leads to the release of high and potentially toxic levels of the hormone cortisol. Her baby can be born also high on cortisol, leading to a cycle of tension and anger between mother and baby that can have horrible consequences for the developing infant. Again, these consequences will be expanded fully later, but suffice to say they can handicap the child for life.

There are other risk factors that are responsible for compromising a child's need to grow and develop in an environment that will enable the best conditions for healthy brain development. I've mentioned above some of those from before birth, but once born, the following can also impact negatively on the developing baby, toddler and child:

- parental mental health issues
- parental substance abuse
- domestic violence
- abuse
- neglect
- multiple carers
- multiple placement moves   Pearce 2009, p.50

All of these issues place the child at risk, and one of the physiological responses to such risk is the unregulated release of cortisol.

The key thing in all this for us to remember as teachers is that when the default setting for a child becomes this basic fight/flight/freeze, fuelled by cortisol bursting through their system, the chances of positive learning taking place are likely to be practically nil. The capacity for positive learning, of course, is embedded long before a child starts to attend school. But for children with the background described above, panic-fuelled responses become the norm. A young child cannot analyse or understand why he behaves in a certain way - he simply does what he can in order to survive.

We know that all behaviour has meaning. Taking the time to ask just what might be going on for a child who is misbehaving is crucial if we are not going to make matters worse through knee-jerk responses of our own.

School starts - so how should we respond?

A response that can be heard daily in many schools is:

> *"How dare you do that! I will not have that behaviour in my classroom - get out! Go on - get out!"*

And once outside, a few seconds later:

> *"Well? What do you think you were doing? What? I don't care! Just think about it - I want a good reason, or else you know what will happen. Well? I'm waiting ..."*

SCHOOL AS A SECURE BASE

At this point the cortisol will be pumping through the system (of the pupil - and I'm sure that the teacher won't be far behind. Go on! Add a smidgin of drama to this exchange, and feel your own pulse rate start to increase!). It would take about 90 minutes for this spike to be 'regulated' - that is, for the effects of the cortisol to be diminished by a re-balancing of hormones. Simple, repetitive non-threatening tasks in a calming environment - counting and tidying felt tips into a box, for example (a process vividly described by Heather Geddes in '*Attachment in the Classroom*', 2006, p.124) could help to restore normality and the chance for meaningful learning, and perhaps even an explanation to take place.

Of course the challenge is - how many schools have a calm space that is staffed by someone who understands what is needed to de-escalate a pupil outburst - let alone that of a teacher? However, as a teacher who is now operating out of a different and more peaceful space yourself, and in a position when you are able to understand your own reactions to pupil challenge, you would be able to recognise the warning signs. You would have the inner strength to respond to impending trauma, and to act in a way to avoid the worst excesses of mindless confrontation.

It's interesting to note recent and very positive moves to deal with children according to their needs. Charlie Taylor, appointed as 'Behaviour Guru' to advise the Secretary of State for Education, Michael Gove, had the following observations to make in an interview in 2011. Taylor was commenting on the extremes of behaviour that can be found in schools, from low level disruption to serious challenges.

> *At the other end of the (behaviour) spectrum, you have this really challenging five to ten per cent of children - and sometimes it's more than that in some schools - who need this really creative, sensitive range of responses to get them back on the straight and narrow. And that requires time and effort and money.*

For Charlie Taylor in his special primary school for challenging children, this includes proper breakfasts in school and peer massages, coupled with firm boundaries:

> *One of the things that mainstream schools are quite surprised about when they come to see us is how strict we are. On the one hand we don't take any nonsense ... on the other hand we are also very responsive to their needs. With children like this, you get to the stage that you give them what they need - not what they deserve.*

And he concludes, over the issue of schools being reluctant to acknowledge that they have issues with behaviour:

> *It can be one of the biggest barriers. Being able to take a step back ... when it's (bad behaviour) in your face and you're dealing with it day to day, you become very reactive. The child does this and you do that and very often you end up feeding the behaviour. It is hard - it does take time and it does take experience.*

And I would suggest that a key element for effective practice in the 'time/ experience' equation is a teacher who is able to closely examine their reactions and behaviour when confronted with challenge.

This reactive confrontation as a barrier to learning is translated into a very different response by Liam Nolan, the high profile head of Perry Beeches School in Birmingham. Talking about his 'respect agenda' to tackle what had been horrendous behaviour when he took over as head, he said, in a *TES* article from 23.9.11:

SCHOOL AS A SECURE BASE

One of the first things I did was to tell staff that if they shout at students I will discipline them. I don't care what the youngster is doing, you do not shout at children. I told the children that if a member of staff shouts they come and tell me. Then I said that if they shout or are rude to a member of my team, their feet won't touch the ground. The messages soon got out.

In 2011 the school was named as 'Overall Outstanding School of the Year', and so I guess this, together with other whole school approaches, must have had a positive impact on both teachers and pupils. How far it has become embedded in staff behaviour will be seen in a few years time. It could be an example of a 'bolt on' solution to challenging behaviour, this time from a head who is supremely confident and well informed as to how staff challenge of the wrong sort (that is, shouting) merely exacerbates the situation. However, my question would be whether Liam Nolan's understanding has really been taken 'on board' personally by his staff and has become part of their way of responding freely to a challenge, or, were it to have been imposed, when this head moves on to another position, might the old behaviours and staff/pupil conflicts reassert themselves? Let's hope not!

Stress for pupils, whether caused by the sort of early life trauma listed above on p.78, or relentless pressures in school, is the single most significant barrier to learning, and left unchecked will scorch through a classroom with destruction and negativity. Our aim is to create a peaceful and holding learning environment that will enhance the experiences of teacher and taught together.

Before introducing techniques to help stressed and challenging pupils find their own inner peace and security, I would like to look first in more detail at one of the most misunderstood areas of pupil challenge and misbehaviour, that is, the confusion between ADHD and Attachment Difficulties, before looking at ways in which these two - and other areas of challenge and conflict between teachers and pupils - can be addressed.

ADHD and AD

Debates around ADHD will continue, but the physiological explanations are worth revisiting. We all have a threshold of arousal that needs to be approached if our brains are going to be opened to new learning experiences. There is nothing intrinsically wrong with adrenaline bursts as a way of keeping us on our toes in life-learning experiences. However, in the case of a child thought to have ADHD, this threshold of arousal is low. Their observable behaviours, which frequently include -

- impulsivity
- hyperactivity
- aggression
- destructiveness
- poor attention span

- are thought to stem from a reaction to this low arousal. In order to compensate for a poor attention span (a condition that ultimately the brain flags up as being life-threatening, as indeed it might have been a few thousand years ago, when our breakfast-seeking sabre-toothed tiger was just round the next corner), research suggests children engage in hyperactive behaviour in order to stimulate brain activity and to try to increase their arousal levels to 'normal' (that is, what historically would have been necessary for survival). The prescribing of a stimulant drug such as Ritalin is intended to chemically *elevate* brain activity and arousal levels, thus *lessening* the need of the child to become hyperactive.

They can then 'relax' into normal patterns of arousal, and learning starts to be possible (it's worth pointing out that Ritalin has also been 'sold' on the playground by canny individuals to those other pupils who want the quick 'high' that this drug can provide).

Have a look at the following. Might Jack be thought to have ADHD?

Six year old Jack is on the Code of Practice at School Action Plus. He has a very low attention span, but will at times shout out answers which are always correct. If involved in group work he will try to dominate the other children, and if his suggestions are not accepted he will disengage at best, or destroy the work of others at worst. Given the chance, he will leave the classroom, and delights in a TA following him to bring him back to class. He has to be first every day in the queue of children to leave the class for either break, or to go to dinner, and will push in aggressively. On more than one occasion he has run over tables, regardless of the work he might be spoiling, in order to be first in the line. At times he will try to 'negotiate' his terms of behaviour - "If I behave for the rest of the day you don't have to tell mum what I did to Daniel this morning ...". At playtime Jack is shunned by the other children, who are intimidated by him, so he will try to spoil their games by running wildly between them, picking up the ball and running off with it, and so on. Jack will also lie outrageously, even when the truth of the situation is plain.

I could go on, and yes, Jack might be given a clinical diagnosis of ADHD. However, this is Jack's brief case history:

- *Single mother, 18 years old*
- *Mother thought to engage in prostitution to pay for drug habit of self and 'boyfriend'*
- *Police/social services alerted by neighbours over issues of domestic abuse, house used as brothel/drug den, Jack thought to be home alone*
- *At three months removed by Social Services to be cared for by maternal grandmother*
- *At nine months returned to care of mother*
- *At 14 months mother and Jack move to an assessment unit for three months*
- *At 18 months Health Visitor finds Jack sitting strapped in a high chair, with sticking plaster over his mouth - "to stop his crying from disturbing the neighbours"*
- *Jack placed with kinship carer - aunt*
- *Evidence that contact conditions with mother are being breached, and that aunt is leaving Jack with his mother over weekends*
- *At two years, Jack placed with Local Authority carer. Placement lasts two months, then disrupts due to Jack's soiling, smearing, and cruelty to family pet*
- *Emergency placement for three weeks*
- *Jack returns to care of his mother, who is now living with new boyfriend*
- *Jack's mother pregnant - sister born when Jack is nearly three*
- *Jack moves to care of maternal grandmother as mother can't cope*
- *After six months Jack returns to mother, who is now 'single' again*

- *Social worker visits home to find Jack sleeping on a bed with curtains as bedding. Sister lying in cot covered in excrement. Little food in the house, with bins overflowing, remains of a takeaway on the floor that Jack tries to eat. Mother clearly under the influence of drugs/alcohol. Transpires that Jack has been 'looking after' sister, foraging food for her. Sister malnourished, Jack little better, both underweight.*
- *Jack and sister placed in emergency care - two nights*
- *Jack and sister placed with Local Authority carers. Jack starts to soil, smear, steal and hoard food, destroy his room's furnishing and toys*
- *After four months, notice is given on placement*
- *Jack and his sister are separated - sister goes to another Local Authority carer, Jack to an Independent Fostering Agency offering therapeutic care with support for education and health.*

By this time, Jack was four and a half years old. He had experienced nine changes in his care, and was now on his tenth home. He had yet to start nursery.
Jack presented with the following emotional states and behaviours:

- *Fearful, clinging, but rejecting any uninitiated affection*
- *Gorges food, but will also steal and hoard food in his room*
- *Bed wetting*
- *Swears and spits when frustrated*
- *Wild in play*
- *Lies frequently*
- *Frequently soils, and can smear - in bedroom and bathroom*

- *Screams when left at night*
- *Plays very roughly with visiting children*
- *Will run off when out of the house - needs constant watching*
- *Can't seem to cope with unexpected treats/surprises*
- *Constantly demanding what is going to happen next*

Jack will go on to try the patience and resilience of his carers to the extreme, but with support they stick with him, and by the time I met up with him he was in Year One - just. Yes - whilst some details have naturally been changed, Jack is real, and the heart-numbing reality is that he is one of many thousands at any one time. Not all Jacks are in care - many still live with their birth families, and many Jills too.

Surely though - once Jack is in a calm, loving and stable home he will respond to this environment and be able to settle into school?

Well - no. Those early life experiences that have impacted so negatively on Jack need to be understood fully, whatever diagnosis he might be given. Repairing the damage done to him will be a long process, requiring carers - and teachers - who are confident and secure in themselves, before he is ready to learn. We will explore further some of the issues around ADHD on p.93, but first we need to feel sure of our knowledge of how attachment develops in the newly born.

Attachment - the vital link?

The gestation and nurturing of infant humans is unique, and has developed for reasons way beyond the scope of this book. Suffice to say, when successful, the emerging human being is confident, happy, able to learn and able to fulfil a destiny that enhances both their own well-being and that of others. This is indicated by the term *'secure attachment'* (first so called by

John Bowlby, who began this work in the 1940's - see also p.91), and develops as shown in the following cycle:

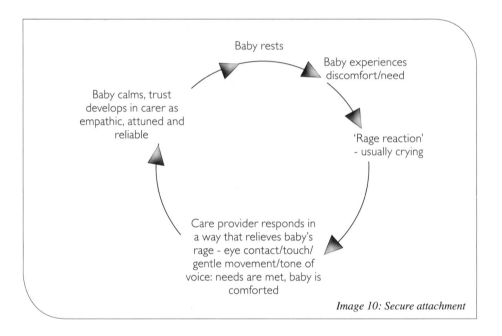

Image 10: Secure attachment

In Image 10 it is assumed that the primary care giver (usually the mother, but there are many instances when another significant adult can successfully assume this role) has qualities of patience, dependability, capacity for empathy and attunement, and feels confident in her relationship with the baby. Out of this a 'secure base' is established for the newly born baby that serves as an underpinning for the rest of his life.

The gentle nurturing cycle shown above is repeated a thousand times, and through it trust builds in the baby - trust that his world is safe, predictable and secure. Not only are his physical needs met, but quite quickly neural pathways are laid in his brain that enable these safe outcomes to be transferred to other life situations. He is able to branch out as a toddler, explore and have mishaps, but always safe in the deep-rooted experience and knowledge that a safety net is always there, and that the world is populated by people he can have trust in.

If we look again at Jack's short life, we can see how his expectations of security were dashed from the very beginning. For him, *insecure attachment* is a reality, and characterised by the following cycle:

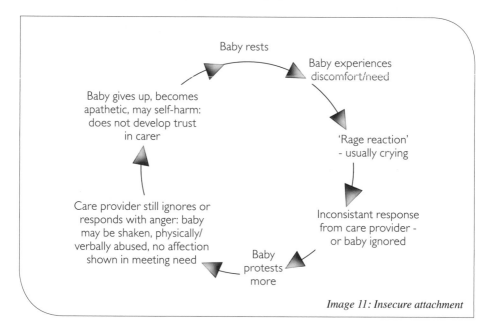

Image 11: Insecure attachment

In this case the primary care giver is experienced as insecure, undependable, impatient and inconsistent. There may be a rapid succession of caregivers, each demonstrating different, but insecure qualities themselves. Sadly, Jack learns that the world is scary, unpredictable and nasty. An elementary survival instinct kicks in, if deep in his sub-conscious Jack starts to learn that the only person he can trust for his own survival is himself. I will detail the full implications of this in a moment.

SCHOOL AS A SECURE BASE

It is quite possible, in any case, that Jack was born pickled in cortisol (*have a look back at p.76 above for the check list as to just what impact cortisol has on development*).

It would take a calm and confident carer to get over the screaming demands of a baby who is born stressed out on cortisol. Couple this with an inexperienced mother, herself fearful of so much, and the chance of the necessary bonding taking place is remote. Jack is going to experience a fractured and terrifying passage into his early years, when he will come to learn:

- physical discomfort is rarely alleviated
- food supplies will be spasmodic
- close contact with his primary care giver will be spasmodic
- uneasiness and panic will be common feelings
- the world is a sinister and scary place
- adults cannot be trusted
- the only way to survive is to look to your own resources
- you have to stay in control

and

- that deep down a part of you still craves human warmth and nurture

Such is the formula for disaster, unless those adults who come into contact with Jack understand the nature of his difficulties and work with Jack to help him develop a more positive view of life. It is possible to compensate for an insecure base, but there remains real risks that individuals like Jack are compromised in their ability to form relationships onwards into the future.

That there have always been insecurely attached children has been documented as a phenomenon, and back in the 1920s and '30s the presence of 'maladjusted' children was recorded and debated. However, it was only with the work of John Bowlby and Margaret Ainsworth in the 1960s and 1970s that the notions of *secure and insecure attachment* were researched and proven. The implications of this work were quickly embraced by social care and health professionals, but the first book to spell out the *practical* implications for education in a practical classroom-based way didn't appear until 2006 (Geddes: *Attachment in the Classroom*). This groundbreaking work was followed in 2007 by a whole school approach to dealing with pupils with attachment difficulties (Bombèr: *Inside I'm Hurting*) and in 2009 by a series of essays by leading professionals on how teens who continue to struggle with insecure attachment patterns of behaviour and relating can be helped (Perry (Ed), *Teenagers and Attachment*). If all three books were to become the bedrock of INSET across the country, I believe outcomes for all schools would improve a thousand-fold.

It takes a well-grounded, secure and peaceful teacher though to meet these challenges head on. And we first need to be aware of just how insecure attachments present themselves in the first place.

So back to Jack - how might his insecure attachment manifest itself in school?

Jack is slow to trust adults, if he does at all. He has come to regard all adults as dangerous, and he cannot hand over control to them

Jack has to stay in control - and he can exercise this by getting adults to do what he wants them to, by lying, running away, and 'negotiating'

Jack has to be first - in case he misses out on food or anything else. If he isn't first, someone else will beat him to it

Jack has to manipulate relationships - with other children too, so that he can have the 'comfort' of thinking no-one will exploit him,

> hence the difficulties of group work and reciprocal sharing
> *Jack will 'divide and rule'* - one bit of 'truth' to his class teacher,
> another bit to his TA and so on
> *Jack is unwilling to take risks,* as he has not learnt how to regulate
> feelings of shame should he make a mistake

Jack is, then, one very challenging little boy (and indeed, very challenged, if we can but see it). If his needs aren't recognised and adequately met, then statistically, the challenging little boy is likely to end up as an institutionalised criminal, who might well have carried out a random knife attack on a perceived rival, after which he is likely to show absolutely no remorse or feelings of guilt.

Jack is emotionally disabled, with a brain hard-wired to survive against all odds - but also against all societal norms. The ultimate plight of children like Jack is movingly described by Camila Batmanghelidjh in her account of so called 'feral teens' in *Shattered Lives* (2007), and in her latest book, *Mind the Child* (2013).

Your move!

What on earth are you supposed to do with this lot? As a class or subject teacher with a six or 16 year old Jack to contend with, how can you make a difference?

To clinically differentiate and diagnose between ADHD and AD lies outside our remit as teachers. However, with the knowledge we now have, we are in a better position to offer informed advice to those who *can* give a diagnosis. As importantly though, we can now respond to patterns of chaotic behaviour in a way that may well give a child like Jack the security he desperately needs. And this will lead to a classroom where the needs of all are met, and so to classrooms where strife and ignorance are increasingly replaced by peace and knowledge. The first move has been made - you know now about attachment difficulties, and you know where you can obtain highly accessible information and detailed strategies to work with these patterns of relating.

Next is the fact that you are still working on what we might think of as your own 'secure base' of peace, out of which can flow so much willingness to stand aside from confrontation, and to question just what is happening in any difficult classroom relationships you experience. None of us can expect to alleviate the problems of a child who may have attachment difficulties single handed; the complex and demanding nature of their mangled lives demands a whole school approach, and support from a range of colleagues, in and out of school. And although it would be unrealistic to expect to 'win them all', we can now avoid the pitfalls that resulted in a no-win situation all round, through developing our peaceful approach.

Finally, the treatment of ADHD is again under fire, most recently from the Association of Educational Psychologists, who have sounded alarm bells over new 'guidance' being issued in America (the widely used Diagnostic and Statistical Manual of Mental Disorders, DSM-5), introduced in the UK in May 2013. The new edition reduces the number of observable symptoms or severity of ADHD, before drug therapy is prescribed. This is against a background of a huge increase in Ritalin prescriptions in the UK, from 155,000 in 1999 to 661,463 in 2010 (Source, NHS, cited in the *TES* 21.9.12). The chances therefore of more mis-diagnosis between AD and ADHD are compounded, and the chances of using this knowledge wisely to help promote peace in challenged pupils further compromised.

Fortunately, whatever happens in this clinical sphere there are other proven strategies that can help pupils whose behaviour suggests difficulties of the kind I've been describing. These strategies build on recently applied knowledge concerning brain development and emmotional security, and will benefit all pupils in any class, enabling them to relax more, learn more and contribute more in the creation of a secure and peaceful school.

SCHOOL AS A SECURE BASE

To the gym!

Movement is the door to learning.   Dr Paul Dennison

No need for trainers - all of this gym work can be done in the comfort of your own classroom, and is based around the movement exercise known as Brain Gym.

Originally called 'Dennison Laterality Re-patterning', (not the most memorable of names!), Brain Gym is based on the research and development of Dr Paul Dennison, who, in his personal struggle to find a way through his own dyslexia and visual difficulties, developed the Brain Gym programme in the late 1960s, synthesising the work of other pioneers from the previous 70 years. The common component was the link between movement and learning, which breaks down the barrier between mind and body. The work of Rudolf Steiner is one noteworthy example of how this link (called eurythmy, in the case of Waldorf-Steiner schools) anchors the learning of children with rhythm and specific activities.

The co-ordinated activities, now known as Brain Gym, are deceptively simple, and build on the processes of any learning situation, through -

* sensory input
* integration and assimilation into the brain
* action

For learning to take place, the child has to be relaxed in order for the brain to function in its entirety, with left and right sides of the brain exchanging information and consolidating new input across the corpus callosum, a dense bundle of nerve fibres that allow this exchange to take place.

However, under stress we find that the impact of cortisol on the corpus callosum may block or disrupt the effective exchange between the two sides of the brain, resulting in decreased learning and growing frustration on the part of children - and us, their teachers! It's natural for very young children to learn through movement, exploration, and generally orientating themselves in a secure environment. And we can perhaps see how children suffering from an insecure attachment will already find their ability to learn in this way compromised for the reasons already stated.

In order to bring about the re-activation of these key stages in learning, Dr Dennison has identified three key dimensions that are addressed by the following processes:

LATERALITY	Simple exercises that co-ordinate the left and right sides of the brain in order for new learning (and learning that has only been partially 'absorbed' into a fully co-ordinated brain) to pass effectively between them
CENTERING	The Brain Gym exercises also help to co-ordinate the limbic (emotional) part of the brain with the frontal lobes (enhancing our ability to make decisions and think critically), thus improving behaviour and learning, leading to -
FOCUS	The child is now able to stay on task, control impulses and think of consequences

So often, the brain is full of the information needed by the child to learn, develop and take the next step, but because of stress, there is a block in some or all of the three areas described above, resulting in under-achievement, frustration and attendant challenging behaviour. By using Brain Gym, children are enabled to have fun, relax, and so, in any case, be more receptive to new learning.

Studies around the world have proved the efficacy of Brain Gym time and time again. In her description of Brain Gym in her book *Smart Moves* (1995), Carla Hannaford describes how pupils experiencing difficulties around learning situations in Russia, South Africa and Hawaii benefited from Brain Gym. In her concluding paragraphs, Hannaford writes:

> Brain Gym is effective for everyone and optimises learning and performance at every level in all cognitive endeavours ... Because the exercises relieve and manage stress, Brain Gym also contributes to overall health ... But perhaps the most profound improvements from Brain Gym that I have witnessed were with adults and children labelled 'learning disabled', 'ADHD', 'Emotionally Handicapped', Downs Syndrome. Brain Gym is drug free, simple and highly effective. It maintains a fine-tuned mind/body system and assists global learning and comprehension for all.   pp.130-31

It is now used in many schools in the UK. Here's one small personal example:

> *Whilst conducting some very demanding CAT tests with a group of Year 7 pupils, I had a break in the middle in which I asked the whole group to stand and perform one of the basic Brain Gym exercises, The Cross Crawl. Whilst I can't vouch for a huge improvement in their scores, I do know that the whole atmosphere and concentration in the second part of the test was vastly improved.*

That children need to move in order to learn can be vividly illustrated by our inveterate chair swingers, who seem to instinctively know that they need to activate their brains by movement. By far the most counter-productive punishment we can give to these children is to deprive them of their breaks, when dashing around outside isn't just letting off steam, but preparing their brains for new input.

> *I worked with one very developmentally-delayed six year old over a period of four months, who would spend as much time as possible under his desk. Twice a week, one to one, we would work together, ostensibly on his almost non-existent handwriting skills. I threw as much of the relevant Brain Gym at him as I could - movement to music, figure drawing, throwing and catching bean bags. We got through miles of wall lining paper, danced ourselves silly - at the end of our time together, the school's request for Speech and Language Therapy was withdrawn, and James was on his way ...*

As well as unblocking learning pathways, Brain Gym brings with it and enhances a range of social skills which all contribute to promoting a peaceful classroom. These include:

The capacity to empathise with others

The capacity for developing confidence and self-esteem

The skill to work both as an independent learner and as a member of a group

The skill to problem-solve

And of course, children who feel skilled and enabled to learn.

The programmes necessary to access Brain Gym are easily available, and the references on p.189 point to two sources that I have found invaluable. If you want to know what Brain Gym looks like, Morecombe and Wise dancing off stage to the strains of *'Bring Me Sunshine'* could be an example of Brain Gym in action - all that cross lateral left hand to right heel stuff, and available on repeats if you can't remember the original! More recently, some of the moves of 'Gangnam Style' dancing have elements of Brain Gym in them, albeit exercised somewhat more frenetically!

Back to the heart

By now, some readers may be practising the HeartMath-inspired exercises (*outlined on* p.51) in Section One. As I suggested then, HeartMath is equally applicable to children as to adults, and has been instrumental in positive behavioural changes in primary and secondary schools - and with pupils diagnosed with ADHD.

It's interesting to note that as Dr P Dennison was perfecting the Brain Gym programme in Southern California in the late 1960s and early '70s, Doc Childre and the HeartMath Institute were rolling out their work in the same area. Did they ever meet? Who knows: but what matters is that both interventions can bring peace and calm to your pupils.

You can use the software yourself and with your pupils to reinforce just what is happening when Heart Rate Variability hits the level of maximum coherence (and it does pack quite a punch to see how you can alter your incoherent jagged on-screen graph to smooth waves of calm coherence!).

It is equally possible though to dispense with the software, and use the basic principles of breathing and creative visualisation (*see* pp.55) to bring a sense of peace and well-being to pupils. The following quotes are from children and staff at a primary school in Co Durham where a whole school programme of using HeartMath techniques 'without the software' had been in operation for a year beforehand, using whole class relaxation techniques at the start of each morning and afternoon session.

From the children:

> *"I feel calmer"*
> *"We are more friendly to each other"*
> *"If something happens in your family and you feel stressed out, I do HeartMath"*
> *"Everyone's calmer and I don't shout at my sister, and my sister doesn't get on my Dad's nerves."*

From a class teacher:

> *"The children are less fidgety, more settled and ready to work. In class they respect each other more, are more friendly and look out for each other more."*

And from the head teacher:

> *"The whole school is a lot calmer now - it's very good on a windy day! The technique is simple, and can be used throughout the day. No-one can access anything new when they are tense and anxious. Its simplicity and consistency of use has had a huge impact on the school."*

I'm not sure that anything can be added to that, but let's shift the focus to Year 11s at a high school in the north-west. The school is in an area of high deprivation, and HeartMath techniques were introduced in the year leading up to GCSEs, with a view to improving exam outcomes. The thinking is that if the brain is less stressed (in an exam room), the student can more easily access all the necessary information to answer the question (assuming it's been inputted in the first place!). The results amazed even those who were expecting to see a significant impact: 100% improvement between predicted and actual grades, translating into an 11% improvement in 5+ A* to C grades (this rose to 21% the next year) (*TES* 25.6.04 and Hunter Kane 2006).

CURE ALL - ADHD AND ATTACHMENT DIFFICULTIES FIXED?

Research using HeartMath carried out by Dr A Lloyd (current Director of The ADHD Foundation, based in Liverpool) with samples of pupils diagnosed with ADHD exceeded all expectations. His work was rigorously monitored and evaluated. To begin with, the spectacular results were doubted and researchers (at Liverpool John Moores University) double-checked the whole study - finding that the results were indeed accurate (*British Journal of Educational Research in Special Educational Needs*, Autumn/Winter 2007/8).

The work to find an alternative way to work with ADHD stemmed from the growing unease felt by some researchers and clinicians who felt that medicating children with psychostimulants doesn't offer the solution that some would claim: that the long term effects of Ritalin, for example, have yet to be determined, and that such absence of information is troubling. There is an unresolved controversy over the link that might exist between childhood use of Ritalin and later cocaine addiction (for instance, as outlined in a 2012 report from the Genetic Learning Centre).

Instead, a multi-modal approach, to also include nutrition, counselling and family support has been proposed (as early as 1999, the benefits of such an approach were reported after a 14 month Canadian study of 600 seven to nine year olds in the *Canadian Journal of Psychiatry* 44.10, 1999), and it is in this context that Dr Lloyd used HeartMath, first with a small sample of eight pupils, then with a larger group of 38 aged nine to 13.

The improvements in the areas of attention, working memory and long term memory through the HeartMath programme were monitored by a renowned independent organisation in assessing cognitive function (CDR Ltd), using a control group who carried out exercises using Lego building blocks, following a programme that was also believed to improve outcomes for ADHD pupils. The overall improvement in the functions mentioned above was 50.8%, as opposed to 3.1% in the control group.

In addition to the hard figures, verbatim reports from pupils, teachers and parents were collated, and what follows is taken from one of these, *Peak Performance in Education* (Hunter Kane, 2006):

From a female pupil, aged 12:
"HeartMath is good, it makes me feel happy."

From her English Teacher:
"She is doing much better in lessons since doing HeartMath, her attention and concentration both seem better. She is less likely to chatter through the whole lesson, and is more responsive when asked questions."

And from her mother:
"Her aggression towards her brother has calmed down a lot and she tends to remove herself from confrontation rather than attacking him. Her sleep pattern has changed and she seems to fall asleep earlier."

SCHOOL AS A SECURE BASE

Motivated by the detailed reports into this work, and with the advice of Dr Lloyd, and the support of HeartMath trainers, I initiated a study in the Independent Foster Care Agency where I then worked. The agency offered a very thorough 'Team Around the Child' approach to care, due to the complex and challenging nature of most of the children and young people referred to us by local authorities; Jack (p.84ff) was one such example, though when I worked with him I hadn't come across HeartMath. Many of these children and young people were on the edge of institutionalised care, and a placement with us was often the last attempt at family life. Each child received the close support of a teacher, a child resource worker, a health advisor and our own social worker, as well of course as the family of the foster carer. Attachment disorders, in their various forms, were the order of the day.

I reasoned that if HeartMath could change the outcomes for ADHD, what about attachment difficulties? We identified families who we thought had children placed with them who might benefit from HeartMath intervention, as well as the carers themselves being sympathetic to such an intervention, and prepared to try it themselves first. We initially trained the carers and support staff, with the carers themselves using HeartMath to begin with. After this stage we introduced it to the children and young people over time, the idea being that the carers would then be in a strong position to model its use to the children and encourage its application.

The big difference between this intervention and all other uses of HeartMath that I am aware of is that its delivery was to be in the family home, rather than in a school, prison, office or other institution. This relied on the dynamic between the carer and the LAC to be such that after school, and before the crowded events of the late afternoon took over - sports, music lessons, playing out, cadets, simply 'chilling', and even homework (!) - the young person would apply themselves to the 15 minute programme four times a week.

And this was the crux of the whole process - that dynamic, and how it could change from day to day. In some homes, the carers didn't embed HeartMath first into their own routines, and at the first sign of opposition from their child, they abandoned it. In those families where the carers had worked on the programme themselves (with very positive feedback about their improved sleep patterns and lower anxiety levels and so on), the results were still very mixed, with one of the most enthusiastic carers failing to engage their young person at all.

However, if we think about the check list on p.90 of the ways in which attachment difficulties affect children's behaviour and attitudes to other people and the world, a lack of trust in adults, and the wariness of handing over control to someone else, figure large. They could well have been responsible for several of the young people backing off and basically telling the carer where they could stick their HeartMath. Of those who got beyond that, the process of them being able to control their breathing and thus the bio-feedback on the screen, had a positive impact.

The jury then is still out. In the case of attachment difficulties, there are so many other variables, especially when introducing it in a domestic setting. However, even in the most unlikely contexts, HeartMath can still have a positive impact:

Jackie was one of the foster care agency teachers, and was supporting 15 year old Claire with her English homework. They were in the front room, and Jackie had just managed to get Claire engaged with the work, when Claire took a call on her mobile. It was not good - Claire's social worker was phoning to say that she could not bring Claire's mother to contact tomorrow, no-one else was available, and so the contact would have to be cancelled. Claire was furious, threw her mobile down and started to pace around the room, swearing in general, and telling Jackie just what she could do with the homework. Jackie said nothing, but opened up the HeartMath program on her lap top, and brought up the basic screen before starting to carry out the exercise herself. Claire wandered over and demanded to know what she was up to. Jackie explained. Curious, Claire took the bait, and was duly connected to the sensor to 'have a go'. After 15 minutes she pulled off the sensor, looked at Jackie and said "OK - let's get on with this English then...."

Finally, one of the senior social workers at the foster care agency, Peter, wondered whether HeartMath could help his adopted son, Danny, 13. Danny had been given the following diagnoses:

- social anxiety disorder
- attachment disorder
- depression (linked to SAD - season affective depression)
- autism

In addition, Danny had attempted self-harm and suicide by hanging, cutting and scratching, and had not left the house for over 12 months. Peter started the program himself, and after a week was joined by Danny. By week three, Danny had mastered the breathing, and by week five, Peter wrote:

"We took a massive step forward. I was able to walk to the shop to buy my newspaper and leave Danny alone for ten minutes. I've got a good feeling about life. Danny might be able to survive".

After two months Peter was able to report that Danny had not attempted suicide or self-harm, and could be left alone for an hour.

"I now live with a wonderful son who is damaged but has hope".

The wonderful thing about our work with children is their capacity to change and confound expectations - if we are prepared to offer them the calm space and whatever techniques are at our disposal.

Watch the baby?

Both Brain Gym and HeartMath, though based on a detailed understanding of the physiology of the brain and heart, and how they interact, are, in themselves, very simple, and can be done with minimal equipment and financial outlay.

The third technique that I would suggest you consider in bringing about peace to your pupils is similarly simple in its process, but will require more organisation and training. Known as BASE®Babywatching, it basically brings a group of children or young people together with a mother and her newly born baby. The children are encouraged to make observations about what they witness in the physical and emotional interaction between mother (it could also be father) and baby, and to relate what they observe to their own experience (*see below*). The children's simple observations and responses to the group leader's gentle invitation to contribute what they notice form the basis of the programme's incredible success in lowering aggression and heightening empathy.

The programme has evolved out of the work of Henri Parens, a survivor of the Holocaust, who escaped from Vichy France to the United States in 1942, being separated from his mother who was later murdered in Auschwitz. In response to these traumas, Parens decided to become a child analyst, working against racism, war and hatred. This led him to studies in the 1980s aimed at trying to understand what might prevent aggressive behavioural disorders developing in children. Based on Parens' experiences, Dr Karl Heinz Brisch,

SCHOOL AS A SECURE BASE

Head of Paediatric Psychosomatic Medicine and Psychotherapy at Munich University, Germany, developed the BASE®Babywatching programme - (the acronym denotes - Babywatching in pre-school and school Against aggression and fear to promote Sensitivity and Empathy).

The process of BASE®Babywatching is deceptively simple, but does require the group leader to have received the necessary training in the technique and its background. The group leader prepares the children first, and then the mother and baby are introduced to the centre of their circle. The class/subject teacher stays with them, and the leader prompts the class with five levels of questions, each building on the other. Whilst this is happening the mother and baby simply react to each other - playing, laughing, comforting, feeding, changing, sleeping. The five levels of questions are structured thus:

- What is the baby doing?
  What is the mother doing?   → **Behaviour**

- Why does the baby behave like this?
  Why does the mother behave like this?   → **Motivation**

- How does the baby feel in this situation?
  How does the mother feel in this situation?   → **Emotion**

- What would I do in this situation if I were the baby?
  What would I do in this situation if I were the mother?
                                     → **Identification with behaviour**

- What would I feel in this situation if I were the baby?
  What would I feel in this situation if I were the mother?
                                → **Identification with emotions - Empathy**

Group leaders are specifically trained and mentored in how to work with this sequence, in order to ensure that their questionning is sensitively attuned to the children's level of development. In all of this, the responses are oral, and nothing is written down or 'tested' in any formal sense. The children are watchers - they do not themselves interact with the mother and baby, and there is no attempt to turn it into a 'child development course'. Once the baby is actively walking and exploring, their participation in the group ends, and a new baby and parent may be introduced to the group.

BASE®Babywatching groups are established across the world: in the UK since 2012, in Germany where the programme started several years ago and also now in Austria, Switzerland, Belgium, Netherlands, Italy, New Zealand, South Korea, Israel and Australia, with other regions in preparation. They can operate from nursery through to Year 13, and the results are consistent amongst the pupils who have taken part:

✓ Less aggressive oppositional behaviour
✓ Less social withdrawal and isolation
✓ Less anxiety
✓ Less depression
✓ Less sleep problems
✓ Less hyperactivity
✓ Improved alertness
✓ More emotional reactivity

All in all, a set of conditions that will bring peaceful calm to classes and greatly enhance the learning readiness of all pupils and students, as they seem to be able to generalise from their growing ability to 'mentalise' (think and feel about) the mother-baby interaction into interactions with their mates in daily life.

SCHOOL AS A SECURE BASE

The following comments are all quotes from the BASE®Babywatching UK May 2013 Newsletter, and refer specifically to UK based groups:

From a groupleader:

"The boys have all delighted in the programme and really look forward to seeing the baby and his mum, and their behaviour has been amazing; no incidents, and their concentration, attention and most importantly observations have been remarkable!"

(referring to a small group struggling with mainstream education).

From a groupleader/teacher:

"Teachers in the staffroom told me "Your class were so mean to each other in the playground last year; even friends. It seemed to be a bad habit. This year they're so different.""

From another groupleader:

"According to the school this is a challenging class behaviourally, but we have never seen evidence of this as the children are utterly engaged and love the sessions ... The children are making good emotional connections between what they are watching and their own feelings."

And finally, in the words of a Year 4 pupil at the end of the programme:

"It has been a great time having you both. I have learnt that babies are hard to handle but fun and loving, and I see that in you."

From what has been described about attachment disorders, it can be seen that BASE®Babywatching is the antithesis of poor attachment, and will encourage all 'watchers' to develop an awareness of how this beautiful dance of secure attachment between mother and baby develops. For those children and young people in the groups for whom attachment is an issue in their own lives, BASE®Babywatching may bring issues to the surface that should be addressed in any case; we can then provide appropriate therapeutic processes for them, that will take root and slowly but surely lead them to firmer ground.

Other roads also leading to Rome ...

Ways for children to access calm are now coming from a wide number of sources, and include the work being done by the actress Goldie Hawn in her 'MindUP' programme (2003). This draws on mindfulness techniques which might equally underpin peacefulness in the home as well as schools. This work is supported by the Hawn Foundation, which launched its own UK organisation in 2012, and is currently delivering its 'MindUP' programme in about 20 schools in the London area. The programme draws on elements of discussing how the brain works, mindfulness exercises, controlled breathing and expressing gratitude. The programme is delivered in a series of 15 sessions, but is then applied to all lessons and school situations. It is interesting to compare the comments children make about the effects of 'MindUP' to the comments made in the school in County Durham that had been practising HeartMath (*see* p.101 *above*) - they are interchangeable!

From a Year 7 pupil:
> *"I love MindUP! It is a way to focus your mind, calm down and reflect on a situation when you need to make a choice."*

From a Year 6 pupil:
> *"Being mindful calms me down when I am angry. It helps me not*

to get in a big fight because I don't want to hurt my friends. It also helps me focus on my work."

And from a teacher:

"It saves the students time, helps student focus and I have more control and patience while the kids are engaged in learning."

One of the international directors of the Hawn Foundation is the world renowned English educationalist Sir Ken Robinson, who has long advocated for the education of the heart as well as the brain. It is also significant that those interviewed on the Hawn Foundation website frequently make the link between the fact that the programme enables teachers to manage their stress levels, thus benefiting the children. In the words of Goldie Hawn, it is all about 'emotional learning supported by brain research.'

When ignorance is bliss ... ?

So much is now known about how a child can best be prepared to learn, in ways that will minimise the risk of 'failure', and the associated behavioural fall out and challenges that can result from that.

The problem though seems to be an almost institutionalised delay in proven research getting through to the 'chalk face' and the teacher. It seems almost obscene that the unavoidable traumas of attachment difficulties are still being inadvertently compounded in schools by teachers who could do so much to alleviate their effects, for example. A few months ago I was sitting in a conference on special needs, and next to me was an experienced teacher from a PRU. We got chatting, and I mentioned the impact of attachment difficulties on learning. My colleague said, *"Oh yes - I've heard about those. What are they?"*

Experience has shown that this response is not untypical. And no - I do not blame the teacher. We've already got ITT, CPD and INSET - so why aren't these programmes more tuned to knowledge that is proven, and to techniques that can really have a positive impact on learning?

Who will train the trainers?

How many more research reports are required before we realise that current teacher education fails to prepare the profession to meet the needs of complex learners?

The opening sentence of this letter published by the *TES* on 18.1.13 is from the headteacher of a special school. However, we know that under the process of inclusion, complex learners can be found in all sectors of education, and that in the case of attachment difficulties there is often the chance that the learning needs won't even have been properly identified. The lack of a child-centred approach in ITT is a real problem, and the emphasis currently placed on curriculum and outcomes is shown by the generic course content from the current Department of Education website. Courses need to provide the following:

- A knowledge and understanding of the relevant national curriculum programmes of study for your subjects.
- Planning and preparing lessons and setting learning objectives.
- Managing classes, promoting good behaviour and minimising disruptions.
- Using information and communication technology effectively.
- Awareness of the professional values expected of teachers, in their attitudes and behaviour towards pupils and colleagues.

It is only at the third bullet point that we find there might - just might - be input concerning how children learn, and the barriers to that learning. Wow! Children actually get a mention! Surely, this point needs further expansion and putting firmly at the head of any list.

However, a more detailed search of the DoE website throws up a tad more detail concerning resources for ITT trainers to use when considering SEN provision on their courses. Referring to the one year primary and secondary post graduate courses it states:

- The resources are designed to meet the tight time demands of a one-year course and include materials covering a range of aspects of SEN and disability designed to provide introductory material for two half days or one taught day.

And in addition to this, there are several other resources that seem to be aimed at self-study should the motivation be there on the part of the student teacher.

So - one whole day in a whole year's course - hardly promising! As a quick experiment I followed the links it was suggested would further the confidence of a newly qualified teacher wanting to know more about SEN and issues associated with it, only to draw a blank a few clicks of the mouse later. It appears that with the disbanding of the Teacher Development Agency, certain web pages have been archived, but not the final links to the training materials themselves.

Despite this, the new Teachers' Standards which came into effect from September 2012 state that, '... a teacher must ... adapt teaching to respond to the strengths and needs of all pupils', and in particular:

> ... have a clear understanding of the needs of all pupils, including
> those with special educational needs ... and be able to use and evaluate
> distinctive teaching approaches to engage and support them.   (p.8)

Noble sentiments, but not a lot of evidence that ITT, or CPD, is addressing the issues raised. When we further consider that it is the DoE's intention that by 2015 well over half of all ITT will be delivered in schools, and that much of this will be delivered by other teachers, we can perhaps conclude that what those staff members weren't taught is hardly going to be passed on to their trainees.

Back in the early 1970s when I completed my PGCE, the work of Bowlby was only just becoming known to social workers, and so it is small wonder that it didn't appear on our course. But I fear that even now, many tutors (or school based teacher trainers) are trying to side-step the question of attachment difficulties and their impact on learning patterns, or even the effects of maltreatment on learning capacity. With this disconcerting lack of understanding, it is equally small wonder that teachers are not being prepared in a way that could do so much to promote effective learning, achievement, and peace in their classrooms.

I would like to suggest that at whatever level ITT is undertaken, there must be consideration given to:

✓ The child as learner - how the brain develops in the context of early relationships.
✓ Blocks to learning - trauma, anxiety, stress, poor nutrition.
✓ How normal development is compromised (including the capacity to learn) by substance abuse in pregnancy: the effects of premature birth on brain development, attachment difficulties, separation and loss, domestic violence, neglect, abuse, autism, dyslexia, ADHD.
✓ Adapting teaching styles to the needs of children with SEN.

✓ Helping to remove stress in the lives of the children we teach - the use of HeartMath®, Brain Gym, BASE®Babywatching and so on.
✓ Gifted and talented - yes, they have their story too: and if their needs are unmet, there can be displays of challenge and frustration that can also be highly disruptive.

For teachers who are already qualified, whether they are long or short in their educational teeth, I would like to see the above developed as a series of CPD modules. My experience and that of an increasing number of collegues is that if you look at and address the needs of the child, the outcomes will take care of themselves!

In the meantime, from our own vantage point of self-examination, of relaxation, of metacognition, we can embark on the mission of bringing about peaceful schools, and we can start to tap into the wealth of support and advice available now on how security and peace can enhance the learning of our pupils.

Section two

In summary

* We now have an unparalleled wealth of information available to us as to how humans learn and how an environment conducive to promoting maximised learning can be achieved. Much of this has only come online (as far as mainstream education is concerned) in the last 15 years or so.

* We cannot yet rely on this being actively promulgated through Initial Teacher Training, or finding a place on CPD programmes. You are now, however, in a position to:

→ Understand how trauma can impact disastrously on a child's ability to learn.

→ Recognise how misbehaviour might be communicating something about attachment difficulties.

→ Introduce movement as an essential component in successful learning, through programmes such as Brain Gym.

→ Introduce the essentials of HeartMath® or elements proposed by the Hawn Foundation to calm pupils and thus enable them to learn effectively.

→ Consider the positive impact a BASE®Babywatching Group could have on the well-being of your pupils (visit www.babywatchinguk.org).

* Through all of this, the intention is to help children to be in, and to be able to return to a calm state, in order for them to be receptive to new learning experiences, and for them to operate in a social context underpinned by peace and positivity, rather than one fuelled by fear and aggression. Taken together, the school starts to become a secure base which supports the well-being of all pupils - and their staff.

Section three

AN INTERLUDE:
TIME FOR QUESTIONS

Banquo	The earth hath bubbles, as the water has
	And these are of them. Whither have they vanished?
Macbeth	Into the air, and what seemed corporal melted
	As breath into the wind …

And so vanish the three witches at the start of Shakespeare's *Macbeth*. They had made tempting and yet dangerous promises to both Macbeth and Banquo before disappearing.

Naturally I don't want to put anyone off the prospect of peace in schools, but it's possible that everything I've suggested so far might seem, to some readers, as unreal and strange as the apparitions greeting Macbeth, making them question whether what I'm advocating - how we might act and think about the stresses of teaching - would be more acceptable on the moon (or even medieval Scotland) than 21st century Britain.

No criticism is invalid, and at this point in the book, I'm going to pause, take stock and give space to readers who might want to question the suggestions so far; sort of engage in a bit of bubble-bursting.

So from this section, you will ...

✓ Have a chance to briefly review the first two sections.

✓ Think about doubts and questions expressed about the processes suggested so far.

✓ Read a report of detailed discussions held by education. professionals on the theme of 'peaceful schools'.

We don't exist in isolation. Together with our pupils we're part of a complex web of relationships and expectations that go beyond the school gates. As recently as September 2013, a suggestion was made that primary school teachers should be trained to spot mental health problems in their pupils, as a way of trying to stem the growing tide - and costs - of disorders in adults (reported in the *TES* 27.9.13).

This might seem to be part of the problem I referred to at the start of Section One. As teachers, we're expected to deliver an incredibly wide range of outcomes, many of which almost seem to be out of our control. This in itself can lead to tension, and part of what I emphasised in Section One was that we need to learn, if at all possible, not to become stressed over issues that are actually totally beyond our control. However, the whole thrust of advice in Section One was for us to take a long hard look at what makes us tick, and to try to pick out anything within our own orbit that we *can* take control of, and thus begin to generate peace in ourselves.

Section Two outlined proven strategies that we can use in our schools to bring about security and peace for pupils, as well as looking at those areas in child development that can be compromised by attachment issues and thus undermine the child's ability to learn effectively.

I have to admit that since the world is far from ideal, and the pressures for schools to achieve outcomes to keep them out of Special Measures are relentless, all these strategies can be challenged, whatever success I and many others have already experienced in promoting peace and stability amongst teachers, pupils and their schools. It's a wonder all the goal posts we have to deal with are still standing up, they are moved so frequently! When an OFSTED inspector was asked what he thought of Babywatching, for example, his reply was brutally to the point:

> *(As OFSTED inspectors)... we aren't expected to 'think'. If it (BASE®Babywatching) improves demonstrable outcomes, it's good. If it doesn't, it's bad, and you shouldn't be doing it!*
>
> Personal communication

Black and white maybe, but a pointer that for some, unless a 'peaceful school' delivers improved outcomes, the concept is a dead duck!

As a sort of litmus test for the whole process of bringing peace to schools, I helped to plan and lead a workshop in Birmingham on this theme of school as a peaceful and secure base, with a wide cross-section of education professionals. In order to touch base on how the ideas I had put forward during the morning session might be received by schools, we held a lively debate, with a widely experienced primary head and myself. It had not been rehearsed and the questions and challenges he put forward were real enough. What follows is an attempt to capture that session … and what took place between us might well mirror some the reactions you too have experienced as you have been reading this book.

Head teacher (HT)

> *You've put forward some interesting ideas, but how would you respond to someone who thought that the whole notion of a 'peaceful school' was misguided?*

SCHOOL AS A SECURE BASE

Kevin Street (KS)

So much depends on who that person was, their position in a school, and whether they were questioning such a concept in a primary or secondary setting. Hopefully, questioning is going to be based on an understanding as to how humans best learn, and how the brain is thought to work. If their concept of 'peace' is one of woolly niceness, and that children need stress in order to strengthen them for the 'real world', we would have to have the 'greenhouse' discussion - that hardy annual plants are rooted and grown in a well-controlled, protective environment. Just like children, they are going to have to exist in outside conditions that are far from ideal, but to prepare them for that the plants initially need nurturing.

The analogy to schools should be obvious. If a child's outlook on life is to be informed by a balanced upbringing, we need to take note of everything that is now known about how this process is achieved, and strive to supply the optimum conditions for learning, in the broadest sense. The etymology of the word education - educare - to lead out - is a pointer here. Even in a 'gentle' school, stress is inevitable, but to allow it to poison the developing individual is just wrong when we have the antidote: relationships with empathic, confident, calm adults, who are intent on creating a secure and peaceful environment.

Within primary schools much is being done already to promote the kind of atmosphere which enables children to thrive, and the growth of Nurture Groups is one example of this. Teachers see themselves far more as teachers of children (as opposed to teachers of subject), though the last couple of decades have seen this ideal sorely tried in the land of league-tables.

Once children turn the arbitrary age of 11, a switch seems to be flicked in society's attitude to assume that by now, their emotional life is somehow taken care of, and that from now on, the onus will be on 'proper learning'; subject-based, and taking few prisoners. I know this is a caricature, but my experience is that much of it still holds sway. But studies of teenagers' brains shows that the development of the neo-cortex and the frontal lobes is not really over until the late teens and early twenties, and until then it is counter-productive to assume that children and adolescents in secondary have 'grown up' brains. Even a teen's seemingly bottomless desire to sleep in late has now been placed in an evolutionary context, and the few schools that have bitten this bullet and re-organised their school days accordingly have noted a marked improvement in outcomes.

But whatever the secondary regime that prevails, the responsibility and expectations of the subject teachers remains high, and unless they can find their own inner core of peace, their well-being - and the subsequent progress of their classes - will be compromised.

I guess all of this would be my response to anyone who questioned the whole validity of an emphasis on the creation of peace underpinning a successful school.

HT   *OK. However, if we look at the three images you proposed earlier (see p.11-12), I feel you have missed a vital point, and I would suggest this third image is more relevant (overleaf).*

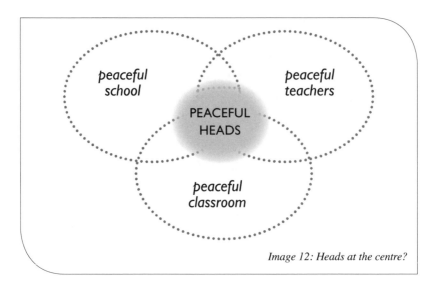

Image 12: Heads at the centre?

You see, I believe that the head is the centre of any school, and indeed the whole focus of OFSTED is on the school and its outcomes, and on how the head is ultimately responsible for ensuring that these are as high as possible. Therefore, doesn't a peaceful school depend on the head?

KS   *I couldn't agree more - that the head, and through him or her the SMT and so on, are so crucial to setting the tone of what goes on. The weekly column in the TES by Michael Kent is eloquent testimony to this, and I recently visited one West Midlands secondary school where much of what I have so far discussed is a reality, due to the inspirational leadership of a head. Ten years ago he inherited a school that was only 60% subscribed - and is now one of the most over-subscribed schools in that local authority. Heads remain central to so much of this.*

But heads move on, and what can a teacher do if they are in a school where the head is marching to a very different drum beat? This too is a reality, and much of what I have so far suggested is aimed at such situations, to enable teachers to become their own 'islands of peace'. Secure and peaceful teachers bring about secure and peaceful children, and peaceful children achieve far more than those who are stressed and unhappy.

HT *But what happens when a head who is fixated on improving sub-levels meets the teacher who wants a more peaceful and secure classroom, school or whatever? Can both of these focuses work in harmony?*

KS *I don't see why not. The whole point about creating a peaceful learning environment is that children learn better, and therefore the measurable outcomes should be there. Look at the example I gave you above of the over-subscribed - and now very peaceful - school in the Midlands. And again, one of the happiest, most peaceful, primary schools I visited to support two very disturbed brothers was led by a head who put the well-being of staff and pupils first, and somehow, all else followed, including a glowing OFSTED inspection.*

A teacher who is being hounded by a head to 'get the results' needs every ounce of personal peace they can get. My experience shows me that teachers' personally won peace will transfer into the classroom atmosphere and the children will start to achieve more. Result! Techniques such as HeartMath® and Brain Gym can be introduced into any classroom, though the wider their use, the more beneficial to the whole school community.

HT *Hopefully, yes. But finally I'd like to focus on the question of peaceful classrooms themselves. In any one class there may well be a number of pupils who would benefit from something like HeartMath, but there will be the other 25 or so who are perfectly OK. What about them?*

KS *Even if there are only a handful of individuals in a classroom who need more security and peace, then the knock-on effect of their disruption on the learning of the others if they are not 'dealt with' is all too well known. And how can we best deal with whatever disruption they bring with them, disruption to both their own learning and that of others around them? We know the effects of cortisol on the nervous system and on the learning process, and far more time will be wasted in classrooms by trying to 'discipline' such children using inadequate, traditional techniques. Isn't it much better to permeate the whole atmosphere of the classroom with peace in order to benefit all?*

   Of course, children will still push the boundaries. No matter what techniques you use which yes, work most of the time, there will still be occasions when the line is drawn, and the consequences of stepping over it are clear. Again, though, the teacher who is grounded in their responses, who is confident and calm, will far more speedily resolve such challenges than one who tries to shout and bully.

   And in all of this, who is to say that the learning of the other 25 won't also benefit directly from introducing peace and proven techniques such as Brain Gym into the classroom? They might be achieving already - but how fantastic if they were to achieve as much, and even more, whilst maintaining a happy outlook on learning and life!

The following four themes seem to naturally emerge from the exchange above:

a) Everyone has the right to peace. Is it harder to address this in a hierarchical situation?

b) Can you have a peaceful school if you have one or two resistant staff? As in, *"My classroom is my kingdom and you aren't going to tell me how to operate in it!"*

c) How do we promote unconditional positive regard amongst teachers? And why might it be a good idea to do so?

d) How can we be effective in a short period of time?

a) Everyone has the right to peace. Is it harder to address this in a hierarchical situation, such as the one between a head and an NQT?

If we claim rights, they have to be matched by responsibilities. Whatever rights we teachers claim, our ultimate responsibility is the development of children's learning. So, if as teachers, we want to claim the 'right' to peace, we have to see this mirrored in those we teach - our pupils have that 'right' too. If we don't take responsibility for our own inner feelings of peace and safety, how can we believe we are fulfilling our responsibility to create a safe and peaceful learning environment for others?

As far as the hierarchy is concerned, peace needs introducing in layers, but ultimately, if the foundation layer is sound (in other words, the individual teacher's own feelings of peace are well established and maintained), everything else has a good chance of following. But if these foundations are wobbly, no matter how fantastic the plans are that are being introduced to promote this or that new scheme, or improve targets yet again, results will be disappointing.

Within the whole school, the process of peaceful learning needs to be sustained, perhaps at INSET days, focusing first on teachers, then the school, then the whole community. The use of outside professionals might be considered here.

However, in that situation, a head will need to feel safe enough to leave his or her staff with another professional, and trust that the process won't be too risky, or that the outcomes won't undermine their perceived 'authority' and therefore the school as a whole. If a head is feeling uneasy and potentially isolated, he or she needs to be able to turn to outside support, not from anyone who might be judgmental but from someone who has their own experience of a head's role, and is able to empathise readily with the demands such a role brings.

If at the end of the day, the head's attitude and approach is a sticking point, individual teachers can still do much in their own areas to promote an agenda of peace, perhaps implicitly rather than explicitly.

b) Can you have a peaceful school if you have one or two resistant staff? *"My classroom is my kingdom and you aren't going to tell me how to operate in it!"*

The answer here has to be on an individual basis - by definition, we can't bludgeon a cynic into accepting peace! We need to try to open up a discussion as to why this person feels threatened, or, if it's obvious, why they are so discontent with their job/kids/school. The concepts underlying bringing about security and peace are not advanced by pushing through the agenda regardless of any opposition. Suggestions can be made, but ultimately manifesting our own peaceful approach and so on will have the biggest impact - as will the changed behaviour of our pupils and the results they are now achieving.

The whole point of the peaceful and secure school is this ethos and what it achieves. The route by which we get there is secondary, and can be varied according to the staff involved, so long as the steps taken build on the same peaceful spirit.

However, that being said, the use of positive language can be helpful to 'nudge' resisters into a more accepting attitude. An INSET course on 'Promoting Positive Behaviour' might have the same principles behind it as a course on 'Managing Challenging Behaviour', but the assumptions of the first will have a more positive impact on people before they actually sign the course attendance register and start the day's training than if the language used is couched in aggression and challenge. It is a part of the 'glass half full/half empty' syndrome.

c) How do we promote unconditional regard amongst teachers? And why might it be a good idea to do so?

The use of positive language can be taken further in our daily interactions with colleagues, again using our own peaceful base as a starting point. Unconditional regard for our colleagues has its roots in our own self-acceptance. We have to be prepared to show our own vulnerabilities, and in sharing them we get to find out who our like-minded colleagues are.

We don't want to be seen as a do gooders, but if our concern for the well-being of colleagues is authentic, they'll genuinely gain from our positive and peaceful support. The use of empathy, of our own positive visualisation, of gently asking them what their ideal outcome would be, of humour … all these will help to create an atmosphere in the staffroom that will be uplifting for all, and will spill out into the rest of the school.

> *"I imagine it must have been frustrating for you when 8G acted like that after all the thought you'd put into the lesson. Would it help if next week you had a word with the PE staff to see if the class could*

get to you on time, and then there won't be such a rushed start to the lesson? I know that Dave wouldn't have intentionally run over, but you know how enthusiastic he gets once he's out on the field. Still, the great thing with 8G is that they seem to be able to come to each of your lessons pretty much bright eyed and bushy tailed, so I know that it will be fine next time you meet up with them ..."

We all have our off days, and we do have to acknowledge, however regretfully, the most peaceful of colleagues may see red and explode at a child. How this is resolved in the classroom is one thing. But in the staffroom, it should be possible for teachers to share their experiences with colleagues, and receive their non-judgmental support and advice. This will enable our colleagues to both explore ways in which they can build appropriate bridges with a pupil who was at the receiving end of the explosion, and also to come to understand a little more what triggered their ire in the first place. This will enable them to reflect on more constructive strategies the next time. And if this starts happening amongst the staff, how much more quickly will it permeate classrooms and the way that pupils will begin to deal with each other.

Hopefully, it is now pretty obvious as to why it is a good idea to promote such support and unconditional regard amongst our colleagues. Our fellow teachers might be having difficulties tapping into their own depths of security and peace; we can still offer them understanding in our dealings with them, and help them feel supported in a school community that values their work.

d) How can we be effective in a short period of time?

In other words, what one thing can I do when I get back in school having read this book?

✓ It might be making a personal approach to a colleague with whom
   you have an unspoken issue.
✓ It might be making a personal resolve to think in a positive way
   about one pupil who challenges you.
✓ It might be including any aspect of what you have read so far (or will
   go on to read) on a staff/departmental/year group meeting agenda.

And thereafter, we could look for ways to ensure that the secure and peaceful
school appears on every staff meeting agenda.

Non-teaching staff are crucial players in this process; what happens at
lunchtimes and around the school is as critical as what happens in classrooms.
At the West Midlands school I have referred to already (p.122), all adults working
in the school expect the pupils to recognise and respect them as people who
have a genuine concern for their safety, well-being and happiness. This requires
investment in the training of 'support' staff, and anyone else working in the school,
so they can demonstrate consistency alongside the teaching staff, and are in
themselves able to show a peaceful and calm approach in all situations. For *all* staff,
unconditional regard amongst themselves is the cornerstone to peaceful working.

The results, again, are wholly positive, with Year 7s never being certain as
to who are 'teachers' and who aren't. And why would they need to be? Within
a secure and peaceful school, all adults are positive role models, no matter what
their job titles are.

For each person reading this, there might be a different set of questions.
Online you'll find a Peaceful Schools Forum on which questions, successes,
cries for help and tried techniques are openly shared. Further details are in
Appendix 2 on p.190.

Having taken a break, the bell sounds, and it's time for us to move on. Section

Four will look at ways in which our classroom environment can support a peaceful and secure learning base, and Section Five will look at the whole school, and what might be achieved if the leadership is sympathetic to this approach.

Section three
In summary

* ★ It's only natural - and indeed healthy - to question anything new. In this Section, the actual concerns and caution of practising teachers have been addressed, shared and answered in a way that:

* → Emphasises, once again, the central importance of the individual teacher.
* → Accepts that in some schools it will be necessary for a few individual staff to 'trail blaze' without SMT support.
* → Accepts that when a head is supportive, changes can be magnificent
* → Links improved outcomes with staff who are calm and confident.

* ★ There is no 'magic bullet' in this, and we have to address the institutionalised habits of a lifetime if positive peace is to become the bedrock of our educational hopes. However, the problems have been recognised, and realistic solutions are possible, supported also by the new online 'Peaceful Schools Forum'.

Section four

BRINGING PEACE TO CLASSROOMS

It was such a crowded scene, and there were so many objects to attract attention, that, at first, Nicholas stared about him, really without seeing anything at all. By degrees, however, the place resolved itself into a bare and dirty room, with a couple of windows, whereof a tenth part might be of glass, the remainder being stopped up with old copy-books and paper. There were a couple of long old rickety desks, cut and notched, and inked, and damaged, in every possible way; two or three forms; a detached desk for Squeers; and another for his assistant. The ceiling was supported, like that of a barn, by cross-beams and rafters; and the walls were so stained and discoloured, that it was impossible to tell whether they had ever been touched with paint or whitewash.

(*Nicholas Nickleby*, Charles Dickens)

The colour of the walls, the amount of natural light and the degree to which classrooms are personalised can all affect pupils' progress and test results. The observation revealed that 73% of the variation in pupils' performance could be explained by environmental factors. In fact the difference between the academic performance of an average pupil in the worst classroom, compared to that of a pupil placed in the best classroom, was equal to the average improvement of a child during an entire academic year.

TES 15.2.13, referring to research by the University of Salford

Dickens' eye for detail when writing about Victorian squalor is rightly renowned, and happily for us in the early 21st century the worst excesses of this school scene are consigned to history. I don't think that it should surprise us to learn that the physical environment of the classroom has a direct bearing on the well-being of pupils and staff. The results of the 2013 research, however, may be startling.

Happily, this is an area of intervention that we can actively embrace. When our intention is to make the surroundings more peaceful, quite small improvements can bring about a dramatic change in enabling our pupils to feel more secure, and and thus more able to learn.

In this section, you will learn ...

✓ That the physical environment impacts strongly on pupils.
✓ That solutions to dingy classrooms are easy to apply.
✓ That the regard with which your classes hold you will be enhanced if they think you care about their well-being.
✓ That by being in positive control of your classroom, pupils will come to feel secure, and therefore be able to learn better.

At a national conference a couple of years back, a speaker referred to teaching as being an 'art, craft and science'.

> The *art* is being able to deliver in a way that takes the needs of any group of learners into account - that is, knowing your class. The *craft* is having the skills to deliver the lesson content. The *science* is an understanding of what latest research can offer as to how teaching and learning can be made most effective.
>
> C Keates, General Secretary
NASUWT, Birmingham 12.10.11

I might have read all the latest research and findings on the readiness for learning, and I might know seven pupils in my class who need a more differentiated approach regarding oral work - but if my organisation and class control is chaotic, the art and science of my practice goes out to the window! You can perm any combination of these three to see how a balance has to be held between them all in order for you or me to be deemed an 'effective teacher'.

I would suggest that as inspiring as this definition is, the 'art, craft and science' of teaching will only be a reality when we ourselves are 'artistic' and 'scientific' in looking at our own strengths and skills.

In the first two sections of the book I have described ways in which we, and then our pupils, can be enabled to operate from a personal base of peace. It is time now to look at how this might be supported in the daily classroom environment, as we strive to add an actual physical reality to the notion of a school becoming a secure base.

It is true that we don't all have the luxury of a permanent classroom, but there are still techniques that we can use in any situation to help create a decent work space and, more importantly, a decent atmosphere. Some of the worst case scenarios I've come across conclude this section on p.146 - together with practical responses to them.

Beginnings and endings

The class who barge into a room to find their teacher sitting at their desk, engaged in some paper exercise, or fiddling frantically with AV equipment, have not entered an environment that speaks of calm and peace. Likewise, the class that leaves the room in a rush, with the teacher at their desk in a heated debate with Chloe as to why she started to apply lip gloss before the bell went, is taking with them a picture that will be all too readily imposed on their next lesson with this same adult.

The converse of these two scenarios can also happen. The class are greeted individually by you as they enter the room. Class routine is such that your pupils know what they have to do once at their place - perhaps it's coat off, file out, bag out of harm's way, and then engaging in the task which is on the whiteboard - until the last pupil is in, and you close the door.

Unspoken are these words:

"Welcome into my space. You are valued, and I want to help you progress and feel good about yourselves. This is a place of calm endeavour, and if you respond sensibly we can make great progress and have fun too!"

The bell sounds and with good planning the class are ready to leave. You move to the door, open it, and indicate which row/group/table are to leave first. As the class file out, you make eye contact with each pupil, and a few words are exchanged that are as positive as possible - *"Well done for that final diagram,*

I appreciated the way you handled yourself over the homework issue, hope the rehearsal goes well tonight, see you next Monday ..."

And again there are the unspoken words:

> *"I have appreciated our time together. There may have been issues, but they have been resolved. It has been a good session and I am looking forward to our next lesson together."*

But what of the pupil you wish to see individually, once the 'audience' has gone, perhaps? You will still have the opportunity for this with such an ending to the lesson - and if it is a lengthy resolution that is required, it makes sense to find another time (and support?) for this, because your next class is waiting outside, and the pupil is getting understandably twitchy about the trouble they will be in if they are late for their next lesson.

So much for the start and finish - but what about the middle? What is going to confront the class once they are in your room?

At this point, I would like to briefly mention the growing awareness and research that lies around body language. Again, as a 'bolt on', it will have limited value to 'walk tall', but as a mirror of an internal state, what shines through can communicate to a class more than a thousand words. This was the subject of an experiment carried out in Harvard Business School by Professor Amy Cuddy (*TES* 14.9.12), when two groups of people were asked to sit on their own for a couple of minutes. Group One was asked to adopt 'high power poses' of legs up, hands behind the head, whilst the second group were asked to huddle down as if cowed or anxious. Each group were then evaluated during a presentation they were asked to give for a dream job. Those from the first group were much more successful. When testosterone levels of each group were subsequently measured, it was the first group who had much higher levels, and subsequently this had shown itself in their increased enthusiasm during their presentations.

So much for the experiment, but how does this translate into our classrooms? As teachers we have to be aware that we are also a part of the physical landscape of our classrooms, as well as having a more organic living role to play! So, even before we speak, what we actually wear will be part of our pupils' perception of their learning environment. And the cues for appearance have to be taken from a sensitive reading of your own school, and the expectations, protocols and traditions of each school.

Once we've sorted our wardrobe out, we can consider how we move, how we are sitting or standing, how tense or relaxed we are, whatever is happening with us at a bodily level, and present ourselves in a way that will convey to our classes that they can trust us to keep them safe, and that we are confidently in control of our classroom.

How might this be expressed in practice? We can think about the following.

- ✓ Avoid looking vulnerable and disorganised. Walk confidently into the room if the class are already there and you can't greet them at the door.
- ✓ Avoid looking hunched and tense. Try standing in front of a mirror, tense and hunch your shoulders, then relax. Feel this, and repeat the relaxed feeling in front of your class.
- ✓ Avoid isolating yourself behind your desk, but use the classroom as a stage.
- ✓ When talking to the whole class, stand still - but feel free to vary your position for each delivery.
- ✓ Avoid confrontational body language (towering above, facing directly in front, invading personal space) when dealing with

confrontational behaviour. Instead, talk quietly, sit next to, or get
down to, pupil level, and stand at a slight angle to an angry pupil.
✓ Be aware of the fact that teenagers, especially those from troubled
backgrounds, are not yet capable of finely differentiating nuances
of facial expression, and might well interpret a quizzical frown as a
disapproving stare.

And of course none of this need have anything to do with physical stature. In
one school where I worked, the next classroom was used by Anna, about five
foot tall, but able to exert a power in her classroom presence that was enviable.
She exuded a quiet confidence, a serious sense of humour and a genuine love for
her subject - and her pupils. She stood tall in every lesson!

Naturally this kind of simple use of positive body language on its own is
not enough. But if you have some knowledge of it and are willing to experiment
with making small changes, it can go a long way towards projecting a secure and
peaceful confidence from you to your pupils - as long as it is well rooted in your
own sense of well-being.

Cut the clutter!

The design of new schools in recent years has moved away from the architect's
blueprint that seemed to be used quite a bit in the last century that resulted in
a certain brutalism in approach. That might have been fine in some contexts,
but not for a building to welcome young people. The former Birmingham City
Library is in a similar style, prompting Prince Charles' comment, in 1988:
"This looks like a place where books are incinerated, not kept', and so to
borrow this comment: all too often, when we look at our school premises, we
might find ourselves thinking - *"This looks like a place where they punish
kids, not respect them!"*

SCHOOL AS A SECURE BASE

However, most of us will have no choice as to the design of the building where we spend a good part of our working, waking hours. And within this building are the classrooms themselves - often under-heated in winter, over-heated in summer, poor sound insulation, hopeless acoustics, windows that were last cleaned two years ago, furniture well past its 'best by' date ... the dismal lists stretches on. Just what does this convey to our pupils?

If we step out of the state school system for a moment and step into a Steiner-Waldorf school, we will find classrooms that are painted in colours thought to be supportive of a child at a particular stage of their learning. The researchers from Salford University, whose work was quoted at the beginning of this section, also concluded that pupils benefited when wall and floor colours had been carefully considered, with warm colours complementing the extroverted nature of younger pupils, whilst cool colours enhanced the ability of older pupils to concentrate. Colour does make a difference. The work of Theo Gimbel has been trail-blazing in the healing use of colour, and this concept has been taken up by several mainstream hospitals and hospices, for instance the St Francis Hospice in Romford: can we use this understanding to enhance our classrooms in some way?

Whilst total re-decoration and new colour co-ordinated flooring for your classroom might be well outside budgetary restraints, I maintain there are many very practical things we can do to improve the atmosphere and ambiance of our working space. These include general tidiness and attention to small details, the introduction of plants and the use of music. Such changes will start to convey the right message to all those who come into our rooms to be taught:

"Here is a space that my teachers hold in their awareness in a positive way. Their care has permeated this space, they have made it safe, and they have made it as welcoming as they can. It is ordered, tidy, colourful, and respects my presence."

OK - perhaps not in as many words (maybe more like - "*Yeah - it's alright in Room 5*"), but the subliminal messages we pick up from the places in which we spend time cannot be underestimated. The zero tolerance approach to graffiti adopted by some city authorities (cleaned the next day, new graffiti, cleaned again, new graffiti, cleaned again ...) has brought huge neighbourhood benefits (see *Good Graffiti, Bad Graffiti,* Dr Fiona Campbell, 2010*)* unless of course it's a Banksy, in which case city authorities turn a blind eye! Similarly, you can micro-manage your classroom from this point of view.

According to a professor of neuroscience, Dr Steven Maier, from the University of Boulder in Colorado (November 2011), even thinking about how cluttered our environment is can actually raise our cortisol levels, so how a messy classroom might impact on a class of 30 beggars belief!

Clutter can, though, be tackled easily - we can all tidy the piles of books, get hold of plastic storage crates, label and file, make sure our desk doesn't look disorganised - the message will get across to our classes, and lessons will run far more smoothly when the materials we need are readily to hand. Boundaries are being set in a very physical way that speaks of the fact that *you* are in control, and that the pupils can trust you to protect them too.

Peaceful plants

I'm not suggesting that you turn your room into a greenhouse at Kew Gardens, or a biodome at the Eden Project. But the beneficial effect of plants in promoting healthy offices is well documented, and backed up by research from NASA. According to the World Health Organization (2001), indoor pollution is now as much of a problem as outdoor pollution. Houseplants dramatically improve the air quality of homes and offices, by absorbing, into their leaves and roots, chemical airborne emissions from electrical appliances, cleaning agents and furniture constructed from MDF. The payback is that you then have cleaner, more humid air (which is good for general levels of concentration and children suffering from asthma). Even more interesting is recent research (2010) from the Faculty of Science at the University of Technology at Sydney that involved placing plants in classrooms, and measuring pupil progress (in Yrs 6 and 7) in spelling and maths, against a control group in classrooms where no plants were placed. After six weeks, those pupils in the classrooms with plants recorded between ten and 14 % increase in scores compared to the control classes.

And - plants look nice! Most are pretty tolerant (unless over watered), and if visiting IKEA or similar, very cheap!

You could consider:

- Rubber plants (*Ficus Robusta*) - good at clearing formaldehyde
- Areca palms - good at all indoor toxins and humidifying the atmosphere
- Dragon trees (*Dracaenea cane*) - good at absorbing emissions from computers, printers, chipboard and MDF furniture
- And the very aptly named Peace Lily - good at absorbing toxic fumes from glue and paints

Before you run amok at your local garden centre though, be warned - the Dumb Cane (*Dieffenbachia*) is recommended for offices only, and should be kept away from children, due to its having a poisonous sap that causes a swelling of the mouth and throat if swallowed. Not the best of ways to bring peace to your pupils!

Having planted out the corners of your room (and I would also recommend using plastic containers for the pots, rather than saucers, as they are neater and add stability and colour, and make the plants look as if they are meant to be there), some thought needs to be given then to their care. A wilting, brown leafed specimen is not the image of caring peacefulness you are trying to promote. Are there pupils who can help? Do you need to discourage your cleaner from generously drowning the plants every day? Whatever practical solutions you devise, the presence of two or three well-tended plants can bring much into your teaching space.

If music be the food of love ...

Whatever the amorous intent behind music in some contexts, we have known for centuries that certain types of music help to promote certain behaviours. The ancient Greeks, amongst others, used particular musical modes to take troops into battle in the 'right' frame of mind. In far more recent times, brain scans have shown how certain key areas of the brain can be enlivened by certain types of music, giving rise to the so called 'Mozart Effect'. Research has shown that the music of Mozart, and other composers of a similar vein, can serve to create relaxed brain patterns that help facilitate more efficient learning. This has spawned dozens of CDs to be played from before birth and thereafter. Since this effect was first identified by French researcher Dr A Tomatis in 1991, *(Pourquoi Mozart?)* there has been a constant debate as to the efficacy of using music to improve learning outcomes.

As recently as 2012, the charity Epilepsy Action reported two small scale research projects using Mozart in Tawain that seemed to have a beneficial effect on epilepsy sufferers, concluding that further work had to be done to better understand the connection. One of the adjuncts to HeartMath *(see p.100)* is a specially composed CD of music that enhances relaxation (*please see the HeartMathUK website*). From 1997, much of this work has been developed by Don Campbell, who is promoting music as a means of achieving deep rest and rejuvenation: intelligence and learning: and creativity and imagination (1997, 2002). There are also programmes of music that can be played throughout a lesson to enliven, promote concentration, calm down and prepare for the conclusion *(full details are on* 'The Mozart Effect Resource Center' *website).*

The choice of music is not based on an individual teacher's subjective preference but on the correlation that has been discovered between certain types of music and brain patterns. One inner city primary school I regularly visited had Mozart playing in all the corridors, as the head had a great belief in its efficacy. This didn't transfer to the classrooms though, which could be pretty chaotic! And of course this is the point - no-one can make a teacher 'do' any of this, but should you decide it's worth pursuing, CD players are usually readily available, and perhaps the cost of the music can be invoiced ...

S'not MY job!

I'm sure we have all come across pupils who, when asked to pick up litter, have responded in this vein. More than once I've been told that cleaners are paid to pick up litter, remove graffiti and so on, and I don't think such comments came from any altruistic notions of job protection. As part of ending a lesson, when I was aware of litter on the floor, the bin was passed round and I joined in as well, in a quick tidy up before the next class. It just became 'one of those things' we did. But where do you draw the line?

I've already hinted that you may have to buy storage crates, plants, CDs - and can you claim expenses for them? If not, should you still buy them? I'll be quite open here and say that for me, if it meant an improvement in my working/ teaching environment, with the subsequent knock-on benefits to the classes I taught, I had no hesitation. And I went further ...

Step with me into the mobile classroom where I taught mainly English for three years (in one school, a 6th form student wryly commented, "Why they call them mobiles I don't know. They haven't moved in all the six years I've been here!"). The door is thinly constructed, and the handle on the inside regularly falls off due to there being no hold for the screws. The carpet is stained and worn. Several tables are just holding together, with metal frames/legs parting company with the chipboard tops. Table tops are generously covered in graffiti. The flat roof isn't insulated, and so the room is cold in winter, sauna-like in the summer. Of the three wall-mounted gas heaters, only one works. The room is an odd shape, because an external store room between the two classrooms in this mobile extended into one corner. Rats or squirrels under the floor void have nibbled through the internet link cable. The lights flicker, due to the starter motors regularly failing. Needless to say, the general quality of construction is that of cardboard (reinforced - just) held together with sellotape.

I liked it! At the end of each year I was offered the chance to move back into the main block, but I declined. Here I had no thumping upstairs neighbours, no noisy corridor lesson changes, and to a certain extent I was king of my castle - and this was how I became king. I am aware that H&S might have a risk-assessed heart attack at some of this, and that I will be told by some that what I did was not professional. I was union rep for the majority in the school though, so there was no problem on that front ...

I'm not a qualified gas engineer, so I did make a big H&S noise about the gas heaters - they were repaired/replaced and had lockable covers over the controls so that one person could regulate them - me!

Similarly, I'm not an IT or any kind of technician but I did persuade them to re-route the IT link cable. I put together a basic tool kit, and so when the door handle threatened to come off between periods two and three I could fix it. Similarly I became adept at upending the tables and renewing the fixings that held the legs to the tops

Supporting a cleaner one afternoon we blitzed the table tops. I then assembled a basic cleaning kit and worked swiftly with anyone who chose to communicate their love life on a table top - I sprayed, they scrubbed and I dried off. It took very little time for the message to get through, and once clean a desk is easier to keep that way.

I purloined a storage unit to help 'square off' the odd shape of the room. I used several miles of bright corrugated display board edging as a basic frieze around the top of the walls. I kept the display boards colourful and relevant, celebrating pupil's work. I added a few posters - but I was careful not to turn the room into such an overload of colour/graphics/display that everything would get lost. There is also evidence that pupils with any degree of ASD will be agitated by too much 'stuff': the concept of 'whitespace' on the printed page (a page layout that is not overcrowded and 'busy') is equally applicable to classroom decoration.

The site manager (though then he was called the caretaker) was happy for me to have a handful of starter motors for the lights - easy job (for me) to replace them.

Plants! I had many and most survived and thrived!

I put up a row of coat hooks at the back of the room. These were used at times by my tutor group, at times by my classes. There were not enough for every member of the class, but they helped convey a subliminal message of order and my respect for the fact they had to lug everything from one lesson to the next.

I crudely regulated summer heat by propping open the classroom door and the fire door at the back to get a through draft - and by then my pupils knew me well enough not to try to do a bunk at the end of the lesson through the fire door - well, most didn't!

And of course, I kept constant vigilance and concern for the fabric of the room - surfaces and walls kept clean, no litter.

What I didn't do was to go down the 'Dulux Route'. I know there are teachers who have come in at the end of the summer holiday and applied the undercoats and overcoats themselves, but I drew a line at that. Why? I've seen the results of some such endeavours and at times they look - well - bodged. The two thirds preparation/one third application rule is so true, but the temptation to cut corners is great, and can lead to 'interesting' final results. It's just personal, what works for one person may not work for someone else. Instead I concentrated on what are essentially quick fixes, and things that could be done easily at the end of the day.

However, I had no problem with my pupils knowing that I 'fixed things' - on one level it might not be deemed 'professional' that a teacher carries out basic classroom maintenance, but as it added to the quality of our working space, I drew no such fine lines. And, as unbelievable as this might seem, a handful - albeit only a few - of pupils volunteered to give me a hand ...

At the beginning of this section I mentioned some 'worst case' classroom scenarios. Have a look at the ones below and the suggestions which follow (contributed by groups of teachers in a workshop), and see what you think. What would your response be, if the idea of creating a peaceful teaching environment was uppermost in your mind?

Classroom scenario 1

You regularly teach in a mobile - flat roof, cardboard walls and single drafty glazing. During the winter it can be very cold, and in the summer the flat roof seems to turn it into an oven. How can you work with this to create an acceptable environment?

SUGGESTIONS

→ H&S appeal regarding minimum and maximum working temperatures?

→ Allow pupils to keep on coats when cold, or remove ties when hot - explain that this is you allowing it, rather than them taking it upon themselves and then it becoming a 'uniform issue'

→ Ask for a room change

→ Keep reassuring your classes that you are not happy with the situation, and that you are in it together

Classroom scenario 2

You teach last period on a Thursday in a room that always looks as if a bomb has hit it when you go in. It is empty before your arrival, and the last class to use it are a Y11 group for whom it is their tutor base during pm registration. Because of having to come from the other side of the school, the class you are due to teach have usually arrived and are waiting outside. What can you do to start this single last lesson on a positive note?

SUGGESTIONS

→ Try approaching the form tutor/head of year regarding the need for you to have the class left in a tidy state

→ Direct the first two or three in the line to straighten things up whilst you either remain outside with rest of the class, or join in the tidying yourself

→ Let the class in, and have a timed tidy-up before the start of the lesson

→ Whatever approach you decide on, let the class know that you do not consider this to be a good environment and that you are prepared to bring it into some sort of order - it's only fair for all of you

I am reminded in this of an eccentric English teacher I had in the First Year of grammar school. Nicknamed 'Spike', he would sweep into lessons and judge the straightness of each row of desks using a window pole. Each boy in the straightest row received a 'Good', a system of credits run solely in Spike's English lessons that translated at the end of each term into bars of chocolate. But each lesson started in a quiet ordered way - after a few moments of frantic desk straightening before he arrived!

Classroom scenario 3

You teach in a pleasant enough room, but the noise from the classroom above you is often intrusive - chairs being dragged around, mysterious thumps and bumps, and, during warmer weather when windows are open, objects are thrown from the upper windows - and the teacher's shouting can be louder than the class hubbub. You have 'made the right noises' regarding trying to get some sort of SMT intervention - but the problem persists. How do you limit the disruption it is causing your classes?

SUGGESTIONS

→ Depending on the nature of the class, ask them to help solve the problem by coming up with legal/workable suggestions

→ Draw the blinds (if there are any)

→ Rearrange the seating so that class face away from windows

→ Keep on with the requests to the head of department/SMT to deliver support/guidance to the other teacher

→ Informal approach, direct/indirect, to see if you can 'help' in any way

Classroom scenario 4

The good news is that you have been allocated your own teaching room; the bad news is that it is a tatty, uninspiring space, with tired furniture, scuffed walls, stained carpet, one light that perpetually flickers, and a teacher's desk with locked drawers - the key has been lost. How can you make this into a suitable learning environment that will support your work?

SUGGESTIONS

→ Go to IKEA and get some decent bits of furniture - to be invoiced of course ...

→ Investigate other desk keys - one size can often fit many

→ Posters, work displays and redecoration

→ Plants

→ Ensure that if the school has a 'repair book' that you fill it in regularly

→ Get friendly with the site manager

→ Keep the room tidy

It is interesting to note the similarities and dissimilarities with my experiences on this one. I've been questioned on the issues of pupils cleaning desks and me carrying out DIY in the light of H&S being more stringent now than it once was. And of course the question - *"Are you paid to carry out such tasks?"* is a regular and of course not unreasonable one. I'd say opinion will be divided on this one, and I'm sure reading this you may well find yourself having more than one thought on the issue.

However, my point is that the peaceful quality of the classroom environment - or lack of it - is one over which you have the greatest control. How you choose to exercise this is up to you. What you decide will be intrinsically tied up with your own self-concept, and just how much you are sold on the ideas that I have so far shared with you concerning your own route to peace and everything that comes with that.

Behaviour advice offered to teachers early in a new school year echoes this. Tom Bennett asserts that if children are allowed to sit where they want, flick the lights on and off and so on, they quickly come to believe that they 'own' the room. Instead he advises:

> *Your room, your rules. In my class I decide who sits where and who moves what. When I know they are responsible enough to decide for themselves, I allow that, too.*　　　　　　　*TES* 21.9.12

This section has focussed on your own patch, but in Section five we move into a whole school context, one which you might be able to influence in part, or one that can be a closed door to classroom teachers, due usually to the head teacher's attitude and sphere of influence. Even here, however challenging, I still maintain that internally secure and peaceful teachers have positive impact.

Section four

In summary

★ It is well worth repeating that you are the king/queen of your castle, and that no matter what other restrictions, dictats and regimes bear down on you, if you have your own class base, you can do so much to improve the learning environment of your pupils.

★ Some of the techniques to help along the way are:

→ Physical control: you open and close the door at the beginning and end of each lesson. You turn on the lights, you decide who sits where
→ Environment: tidy, clean, colourful, green, musical - all of these are features of a well-ordered classroom, and are within your control
→ Quick fixes: a plant here, a storage crate there ...
→ Persistence: don't be put off if a plant is separated from its pot, but replace it and carry on!

★ You are peaceful and calm - your classroom will reflect this. Just add the pupils!

Section five

BRINGING PEACE TO SCHOOLS

"We do try to be a community, rather than individual people working in a school. If you're caring about each other, and looking after each other, you're better able to look after the children. It works both ways."

"I always like hearing colleagues laughing. If they're happy, that attitude will translate into happy children."

Head Teachers talking, quoted in the *TES* 27.7.12

Happy the schools that have these heads at the helm! I have no doubt that there will be bumpy times in each one, but as a foundation for creating a peaceful and secure base from which their staff and pupils can thrive, there can be little better.

I recognise that we can't all take such conditions for granted. But hopefully, given a smidgin of good will from the head, many of the suggestions that follow below for extending peace throughout the whole school will be possible.

So from this section, you will ...

✓ Find out how you can extend your support network, without it necessarily being a part of whole school policy, to enable you to create a more secure and peaceful base for your own teaching and that of your colleagues.

✓ Review the reasons for duty, and learn how this can become integral to the school's learning processes, underpinning the dynamics needed to create a secure base extending throughout the whole school day.

✓ Rediscover the importance of play.

✓ Look again at how we 'meet and greet' our pupils, and how the beginning and ending of each school day helps to set the tone of a secure, safe and peaceful school.

✓ Consider just what can be done to protect the most vulnerable pupils in our school, and bring peace into their lives.

We can debate the following question until the cows come home:

> Is a 'whole school policy' the only way to advance any real changes in the school's learning environment, or can isolated pockets of good practice ultimately lead to a whole school approach, almost by default?

I have so far suggested that a key to moving into a place of inner peace and calm is being able to recognise what we can and can't change. And we started the journey by looking at our individual reactions to situations that could be less stressful if we could only stop and question our habitual responses to them.

We also need to acknowledge that in such areas as our own 'inner life', the changes we can bring about *for ourselves* will often be picked up by others, and can have a far reaching influence beyond all our expectations. The push for 'emotional maturity' on the part of leaders in commerce (for instance, the approaches advocated in David Goleman's *The New Leaders* (2002), and for school leaders in the recently published *Mind Your Head* by David Boddy (2012), points to the growing belief that the positive influence that a well-adjusted manager can exert in the workplace is profound.

But whole school policies on this, that and t'other can only be successful if they become the working model for all those involved. Plenty of lip service might be paid to stamping out homophobic bullying, for example, but if there are a core of staff who secretly hold this prejudice themselves, the implementation of the policy will be compromised.

So it is with the whole concept of a peaceful school. The need for children to be secure, happy and peaceful before their learning potential is maximised is a proven fact. If schools are to respect this and understand it, the move has ideally to come in two directions - from 'the top down' and 'from the bottom up' - and where they meet, we have created the best chance for pupils to have the learning environment they deserve, a secure base that will come to mean far more to them than 'good results'. And at the heart of this secure base, at the heart of what will make the difference are the ones who can make the *most* difference - yes, us, the teachers, as I've been proposing throughout this book.

Security in numbers

If you are to feel peaceful, you must feel safe. A pounding heart, dry mouth and a mounting tide of nausea are not a good foundation for teaching with quiet, peaceful authority, and although metacognition and HeartMath are excellent ways of gaining peace, more remains that can be done. In this section I will concentrate on the outer issues around what has been termed 'structural isolation'; that is, the teacher alone in their class.

What happens is that we often work next to each other, but not with each other. At times the only additional teacher in the class is a member of the SMT carrying out appraisal/observation, potentially menacing clipboard in hand. Teaching Assistants are far more frequent now, but the possible tension between them and the class teacher has been the subject of recent reports (see, for instance, *Teachers and TA's working together in a secondary school - should we be critical?* (Deveccli, 2005), or *Deployment and Impact of Support Staff in Schools* (DCSF, 2009).

The days are fading when for a teacher to 'ask for help' was deemed a sign of weakness by colleagues. It's almost routine advice now for newly appointed or qualified staff to look beyond their own classrooms for help:

> You are not going to do any of this alone. You need a couple of big hitters on the staff to back you up and underline expectations for those who need it. Identify these people early. Choose them carefully. You are not looking for the shouters and bawlers, the excluders or sergeant majors. Look for adults with great relationships, the ones the children never try to confront.   Paul Dix in the *TES*, 7.9.12

I believe that one way forward is for all teachers to organise themselves into *support groups* that exist at a level of mutual respect, are non-hierarchical, and are created by the teachers themselves, not imposed from elsewhere.

> *Although it was not created as a support group, I was part of a staff barber shop singing group in one school where the reorganisation*

into a split site single school from three separate schools regularly hit the heights of pure farce. We met once a week at lunch time to sing, mainly for the fun of it but also to give occasional performances. We were a mixed bunch in terms of experience and departments, but we had a laugh, a sing, and gradually we started to tune into each other's wider concerns, needs and triumphs around the school. I can't recall now whether it was specific advice, or the general support of the whole group, but what had become a nightmare Year 9 class I took for English immediately following our lunchtime singing sessions became a class I could work with positively, feeling a great sense of peace and freedom as I taught them.

I'm not suggesting singing as a pre-requisite for a support group, but the way in which my tension levels, with the attendant adrenaline and cortisol playing havoc with my ability to communicate to my Year 9s successfully, were regulated by this particular group is a strong indication that groups can help the individual deepen their sense of well-being and peace. The fact I could relax within the group, feel valued by them, and feel their sympathy for my plight with the Year 9s were all important elements that combined to help me.

It was, in one sense, pure luck that we all hit it off, but the key to any successful support group has to be the people in it, and the fact that *mutual respect* exists between the group members. We all have friends on the staff. But relationships in a support group have to be more than that, though friendships can play a part. When you're thinking of who on the staff group might be someone you could turn to for support, you have to have a genuine respect for the other person - their strengths and weaknesses, their success and failure. This respect is rooted firmly in our shared human experience, of wanting to do 'the right thing' for the children we teach.

The kind of support group that will help develop peace throughout the school community is likely to have the following features:

- ✓ The group will be non-hierarchical. Those in your group might be younger or older than you and hold posts of responsibility but for the purposes of the support group, everyone is 'equal'. There will be no pulling rank or condescension. When we join or invite someone to join such a group, it implies that we are all able to work in a collegiate way.
- ✓ It won't be imposed. An edict from the head ordering the formation of groups is counter to the whole impulse. Support groups will arise out of our wishes, what we're hoping to develop, or they won't happen at all.

So then - once you've identified who you might like to have 'on your team' - what does a support group actually do?

- ✓ It exists to support and encourage. Its members might decide to meet regularly in a location that is mutually comfortable, in or out of school. Such meetings are to share and suggest, not to plan lessons. It might hold elements of peer mentoring, as suggested in Section One (see p.37). A support group could also become an ideal forum for teachers who are faced with the challenges of working with pupils who appear to have attachment difficulties, and need the kind of input outlined by Louise Bombèr in *Inside I'm Hurting* (2007, pp.73-78)

✓ A support group exists as a visible expression to pupils that
   teachers are not isolated, and that 'authority' is shared. What
   does this mean? By mutual consent (of the teacher and their
   group), a pupil who decides to challenge an individual teacher
   is held by the support group. This could be a member of the
   group taking the pupil into their class for the rest of the lesson,
   or a member of the group meeting with the teacher and pupil
   to help decide on the best way forward. Such initiatives further
   demonstrate to all students that their teachers co-operate with
   each other across subject boundaries, and can't be 'picked off'
   individually.

All the above will likely have to operate in the context of existing structures, some of which might have such rigidly ordered approaches to discipline that the second function of the group doesn't appear at first sight to have space to be allowed to breathe. However, rather than invalidating the role of the support group, such a system will actually benefit from the mutual co-operation of teachers. Ultimately 'discipline' will become seen as a way of promoting positive behaviour, rather than a means of trying to stamp out negatives.

We can get a group like this off the ground in a number of ways. In some schools, it could be the head who is sufficiently secure, who encourages and facilitates but does not dictate. In others, it could be helped along by a sympathetic Ed Psych. Where you feel strongly that you need something like this, a group might be created spontaneously.

I'd like to be point out that a support group is *not* -

✗ A moaning shop. It can be that frustrations are vented, but if all
   it does is to chase its own tail on this one, it will soon become a
   stale, negative group of dwindling potential and benefit

SCHOOL AS A SECURE BASE

✗ Just a 'beer and skittles' social gathering, though this might be a small part of it
✗ The place to scheme and plot
✗ A closed shop - others might join by consent of those already meeting
✗ A secret society - though there has to be an understanding of confidentiality, and a respect for the vulnerability that some in the group might feel
✗ Opposed to studying together

John Hattie has similar views, and states:

> Teachers aren't as good as they could be at knowing each other's impact and working with each other to change that. Very rarely do they talk about their teaching, it's all about curriculum, assessment and students. Too many teachers believe that the essence of their profession is autonomy. We hardly ever get together to look at each other's teaching.   Quoted in the *TES*, 14.9.12

And although the essence of the support groups I have outlined is multi-disciplinary, part of an OFSTED report on excellent English teaching touches on elements that can be features of any group. Such teaching:

- shares best practice
- is collaborative
- discusses the methodology rather than administration
- learns from each other
- observes each other's lessons and teaches together

Excellence in English, 2011

The number of traditional school boundaries a support group crosses is in itself important, and can be the start of a new approach to the challenges we face, drawing on the most powerful resource of all - ourselves!

From the stability, co-operation and sense of peace engendered by us working together in a successful support group, it is only a small leap to considering how our schools might become more secure and pleasant, by stepping out together when the bell goes for break time ...

Duty

For duty duty must be done
This rule applies to everyone
And painful though that duty be
To shirk the task is fiddle-de-dee ...   W.S. Gilbert - *Ruddigore*

The 'bits' in between lessons can have a profound impact on the lessons themselves. We have all experienced receiving a class back after break or dinner, when they are 'high'!

Whatever has happened - a fight, a rumour of a fight, an argument with a lunch time supervisor, bullying, windy weather - they are now on the edge of feeling insecure. As a group their ability to settle and focus is compromised by the adrenaline and cortisol charging through them, and their restless, twitchy reactions seem to trigger each other off.

With luck, you will be able to calm them with a quick session of HeartMath or Brain Gym, and acknowledge that the detailed introduction to the new topic you had planned is going to have to be modified. And even if your post break or dinner class is not particularly distracted by a specific incident, if individual pupils have spent this time feeling insecure and vulnerable, their ability to engage is likely to be have been compromised.

On the other hand, I imagine all of us have also experienced a class for whom the break time experience has been positive, and they are now refreshed, renewed and re-motivated, and able to dip into the pool of peace and security your classroom always provides, and able to focus quickly on you and the lesson ahead.

In this section, we're going to look at how we can build such positive breaks into each school day, and not rely on chance alone for a peaceful outcome. We'll start with the logistics of 'going on duty', and then look at how we can best organise the spaces and activities we offer to our pupils.

Here again is a dilemma. How much should we relinquish supervision of the 'bits' of the school day which are perceived as onerous, especially if we find ourselves bemoaning the state of the pupils after break or dinner? This could be a potential minefield. Do pupils have open access to tutor bases during their so-called 'unsupervised time', or is there a lock out, unless the third Ice Age is threatening? We really do need a break, but at what point does that become counter-productive when, as a result of our absence from the dining hall or playground, pupil behaviour degenerates, and the rule of the jungle becomes the order of the day?

One of the happiest schools I taught in had 'falling rolls', and so, with hardly more than 300 pupils, it was possible to know most of them by sight, and many by name. Duty here was almost (!) fun, and marked a healthy social interaction between staff and pupils. This was very different in my next school of 1500, with two distinct buildings, upper and lower school, where even as an experienced teacher I was at a disadvantage when trying to identify who was in what building and why. The analogy of trying to keep water in a sieve was very apt.

Some schools seem to rely on a few senior staff, supplemented by lunch time supervisors, who might be doubling up as TAs, and who might or might not command sufficient respect from those they have to 'supervise' to ensure that the pupils feel secure and safe with them, believing that the supervisor will act towards them in an impartial and fair way.

If we are to work in secure, safe and therefore peaceful schools, the whole issue of pupil supervision during breaks and lunchtimes has to be rigorously addressed, and no area should be unofficially declared a 'no go' zone - for staff.

I was once advised that, when visiting a potential new school, whatever window dressing was wheeled out to the candidates, I should look in the boys' toilets. In the classic film *Gregory's Girl*, a short scene is set in the toilets, which are shown, tongue in cheek, as a social club - cards, chess, wheeler-dealing, and one lad smoking a pipe - but all in a very civilized way. Hm - even this now seems to come from an age of innocence.

But I repeat the assertion - no area of any school should be closed to adult care and concern. New builds take this to the realms of unisex toilet cubicles opening out into a shared wash basin area, and visible from the corridor. Indeed, new builds are often designed so that there are no 'closed areas' and no corridor blind spots. But the reality for most school staff is very different. A maze of corridors, outside areas that are isolated and hidden, 'sandwich rooms' with steamed up windows and messy floors ... all conspire against the creation of schools as secure bases, in which all pupils can feel attached, held and valued.

This is a good start to a list of problems and pitfalls, and I'm sure your own experiences will throw up many more - but can a negative situation be turned round? My experience suggests it can, given that we as teachers are now sufficiently at peace in ourselves (Section One), have a confident understanding of the development and learning needs of our pupils (Section Two), can work in civilised pleasant classrooms (Section Four), and feel that there are pockets of support we can turn to should we feel the need (*see above*).

SCHOOL AS A SECURE BASE

I suggest the following elements can be considered as starting points for looking again at 'duty'.

→ This may 'just' be an exercise in semantics, but could we find another name for 'duty'? W.S. Gilbert's ditty (p.159) sums up the strict and often painful necessity of duty, but within schools staff supervision of pupils is part of the care and positivity we want to promote. We could call it Pupil Time, Pupil Care, Pupil Supervision, or even, Recreation. One group of overly optimistic teachers came up with the idea of calling it 'Opportunities'! Let's notice that what we choose and what we discard probably says something about how we view this time and this aspect of our work, and how it impacts on creating a peaceful, secure school.

→ Supervise in pairs. There is security in numbers in one sense, but also it shows the pupils you can't be distracted easily. Whilst one of the pair is addressing a problem with one pupil, the other is still there to be aware of what else is going on.

→ Vary the pairing: member of SMT with a NQT, Head of English with newly appointed lunchtime supervisor and so on. This will have a number of benefits - pupils will see that there is equality in the staff body, each member of staff might learn from the other, pupils will feel that there is a unity in their school, and that they belong to a body that is able to care for them at all times. This will help to build the picture of school as a secure base, in which no one member of staff appears to be valued more highly than another.

→ Post lists around the school as to who will be where - a sure sign to the pupils that they can feel secure because named staff are readily on hand.

And all of this should lead to -

Peaceful playgrounds

> The idea of play in our culture tends to be dismissed and forgotten, except by those who have studied the most recent research into the psychology of learning.   Holladay 2012, p.121

Further back in this book I established that the concept of peace is positive and dynamic, not just an absence of strife. Having established the concept of 'duty' as being something positive and essential for our pupils to feel secure, how might we translate this into daily practice? Elements of what follows can already be found in some schools, but I believe they need to become the norm.

The bell goes - the classroom empties. What might we hope to see ideally? Certainly, the pupils will be able to breathe out, let go and relax. Because no matter how enlightened, peaceful and positive our classroom is, it is a workplace at the end of the day, and as such will impose certain constraints. In their relaxation, there will be due regard for the needs of others, and for the well-being of all. And - each to their own, whether it's activity on the field, something to eat, chance to catch up with friends ... and all within the safety net of a secure, well-supervised and caring school.

How we might bring this about is answered in the following questions:

a) Where do the pupils go?
b) What do they do?
c) Who is there?
d) ... and when it pours?

SCHOOL AS A SECURE BASE

a) **Where do they go?**

It is essential that pupils *move*, both as the basis of physical health, but also as a foundation for their learning. In *Smart Moves* (1995) Carla Hannaford reviews the scientific basis for this principle, concluding: 'Movement is an indispensible part of learning and thinking'. I have already suggested that to keep certain pupils in at break times for classroom restlessness is totally counter-productive, and our schools need to be imaginative in the sorts of opportunities provided for break time activities, which I'll look at below. However, if we use a pupil's need to move as an excuse for a 'lock out' we ignore other basic needs, for quiet companionship, warmth and security for example, none of which are readily obtained on a bleak rain-splattered playground, or in a clamorous dining hall.

At the boys' grammar school I attended in the 1960s only prefects were allowed the privilege of a 'common room', and the rest of us were herded outside at breaks and lunchtimes. A school extension was being built, and a large stack of bricks at one end of the school field acted as a good windbreak, so a group of us formed a 'coffee club' and congregated there at breaks with thermos flasks to relax and chat. After a week or so we were ordered to move, as we could be seen from the master's room, and our 'laid back' insouciance was not part of the school's ethos …

And this can still be the problem today. Other reasons may be given for keeping pupils out of classrooms at breaks. Until a couple of computers were installed at the back of my tutor base, it had been OK for my tutor group to use the room at breaks, but then came the proviso that unless I was present, pupils had to stay out. It can be the old knee-jerk reaction based on our past experiences, and why should 'they' have it any easier? Put simply, it's because we know now how to maximise learning potential, and that to treat pupils like inmates in a penal institution at these times is not the way to create the best outcomes for our schools.

There is alas growing evidence that in order to alleviate problems at break times, and also to find more time to squeeze in extra curriculum demands, many schools are simply abolishing or shortening break and lunch times. However, on both sides of the Atlantic, this is seen as creating the potential for even more problems. Reporting on research begun in 2007, the American Academy of Pediatrics (AAP) came to some significant conclusions in its online *Journal of Pediatrics* of December 2012:

> We came to the realisation that (breaks) really affect social, emotional and cognitive development in a much deeper way than we'd expected. It helps children practise conflict resolution if we allow them unstructured play and lets them come back to the class more ready to learn and less fidgety.

On a similar theme was a *TES* article from November 2012, reporting on the importance of break times. Of particular interest is Harry Gosling Primary School in Whitechapel, London, an urban school surrounded by buildings and having no natural horizon. Yet the playground there resembles open landscapes, with a grassy hill riddled with tunnels, an outlook post, a trim trail, a quiet area and a football area. There is a PlayPod, a container full of safely sorted industrial waste to encourage imaginative play. The whole bleak playground was transformed in a year following consultations with parents, pupils and staff, and, recalling seeing one boy just walking quietly along the woodland log trail, head teacher Jennie Bird commented, *"There's a therapeutic component to a successful lunch time"*.

And it is the creation of successful break and lunch times that will help our pupils view school as a secure and peaceful place to be.

b)   What do they do?

We are increasingly acknowledging that one size doesn't fit all in a teaching context. So why shouldn't this apply to other times in the school day? Given the need for healthy movement, then some pupils will want to throw themselves into a game of football, tag, skipping or whatever, whilst others will want to catch up with friends, chat and sip hot chocolate. Others still will want to play chess, twiddle with hand-held electronic games, gizmos, mobiles, Notebooks and iPods, or have a romantic tryst ...

This will also be season and weather determined, with more wanting to be out than in during summer/sunny days. I have visited junior schools where the provision of play equipment - baskets full of balls, hoops, diabolos, bucket stilts, bats and so on - has revolutionised the children's behaviour once back in class. This has also been reinforced by training for lunch time supervisors into how such equipment could be best used.

Whilst there's nothing new in this, the wisdom of the few in acknowledging the demonstrable importance of play and recreation for children is starting to permeate general practice. Einstein clearly understood the importance of such activities in enhancing potential when he wrote:

Play is the highest form of research.

quoted in *France Actuelle* Vol 20, 1971)

We might find this to be a bit more of a challenge with older students, but through student councils their wishes can be canvassed and negotiated. When given the chance, the student voice reliably proves robust and sensible, and wishes nothing more for the student body than any well intentioned member of staff would wish. In his book *What Pupils Really Think About Their Schools* (2008), and commenting on bullying (although I believe what he says is equally applicable to any situation in which the student's voice is genuinely heard), Brian Carline states:

> In short, the greater the input of pupil voice into the policy, the stronger the sense of ownership.   (p.132)

and

> Another student council was pleased with their school's response to concerns over toilets. They explained about the need to refurbish their toilets but also that there was nowhere for the pupils to 'hang around' on cold wet days.   (p.144)

Further changes to outside provision can also include 'soft' seating areas (planted, gravel, demarcated in some way), or outside shelters, offering gazebo-like accommodation that can be well used in spring and autumn. In an article in the *TES* of 19.10.12, Dr Aric Sigman reported on the growing evidence that plants and natural surroundings can have a positive impact on pupil behaviour, especially for those with ADHD. He quoted from a study from the School of Biological Sciences at Essex University that found 'every green environment improved both self-esteem and mood'.

So our attempts to improve the outside areas of our schools are going to have a beneficial effect, and add to the ways in which all pupils feel that their school is a nurturing and protective environment, that holds them in a safe and respectful way. The provision of a few covered seats and a grassy bank might not seem a huge step forward in creating a peaceful school, but there is every indication that this provision can have an enormous effect on the well-being of our pupils, as demonstrated by the example of Harry Gosling Primary, mentioned earlier.

c)   Who is there?

All of this needs supervision by staff who are aware of the importance of 'play', and who are on hand to organise and encourage activity with younger children, or with those whose emotional age is younger than their actual age, because of early damaging experiences (Bombèr 2007).

In relation to this latter group of vulnerable children Bombèr points out:

> ... the key adult must not merely be an observer, but an active presence with children with attachment difficulties during the child's free times ... We need to ensure that we do not put these children in situations for which they are not yet developmentally ready ... these childen will not remain at this stage.   pp.214-5

Merely dishing out the play equipment and letting the children get on with it will not bring about the desired outcome of children having a peaceful and positive break time. Instead, staff must be prepared to supervise the games, model good 'sportsmanship', ensure that children are not left out and so on. A sensible balance also has to be maintained here - children should not be so organised that this becomes just another lesson, and once 'up and running', supervisors can often take a back seat.

If some of this work is going to be undertaken by TAs, further training might be necessary, and some extra time built into the day to enable them to have their own 'break'. But in terms of creating a more peaceful school, and therefore a more positive learning environment, we have to see this as a necessary and worthwhile investment.

Flexibility is also of importance here, for the seasonal/weather reasons mentioned earlier. Duty teams (or whatever terms you might finally devise), need to be able to move to where the pupils are, doubling up perhaps if 'their' area is deserted. On a sunny day, when the indoor areas that pupils can access are deserted and the outside areas are seething, it makes more sense for staff designated to the inside to join their colleagues outside, with the occasional check by one member of staff back into the building. This is no easy call, and will ask of us all a level of tolerance and humour that will, however, be richly rewarded in a hugely improved school atmosphere.

d) ... and when it pours?

How many of us have been in a school where two rings of the bell at the start of break means you hold on to that class because of 'bad weather'? Then we supervise that class until five minutes before the end of 'break', followed by the chance for a quick visit to the loo, a slurp of something, before returning to your (steamed up, smelly, damp) classroom. Some teachers swiftly organise to 'double up' (*"Keep your door open, and I'll keep an eye on them"*) for ten minutes each (*"Sorry I'm late back, but so and so caught me in the kitchen - but I've brought you a coffee ..."*), others have a quick turn of dyscalculia when it comes to time (*"Did I really send them out ten minutes early??"*), and whatever the situation, your next class is moody, restless and not really ready for work (any more than you are).

In a school where a more creative strategy is in place at breaks, this scenario is just a distant bad memory, but again, to return to 'The Peaceful Classroom', we can make some preparations for wet and wild days. Your teaching space will in any case reflect your own ethos; it will be secure, tidy, colourful and will meet the needs of those who work in it as far as budget and ingenuity will allow. It will also be flexible in its use of furniture and although the 'default setting' is tables and chairs facing the whiteboard, classrooms are there to be used with different seating arrangements according to the task in hand, and we need to be adept at getting our pupils to quickly re-position furniture.

SCHOOL AS A SECURE BASE

So, the potential disappointment of a class not being allowed out at break, compounded by your own grumpy irritation, can be avoided by having the 'Wet Break Routine' up your sleeve. To begin with, you will bring your class (and yourself) into a peaceful place by perhaps a few minutes of HeartMath or Brain Gym. And then, what else can we do?

→ Smile and sympathise
→ Put on some music
→ Allow a more casual use of the furniture
→ Invite the pupils to eat/drink, with the bin in a prominent position
→ Have to hand simple sudoku, crosswords, age-appropriate puzzles and quizzes
→ Facilitate IT access if possible
→ Remember to have a bottle of water with you in class, and perhaps an emergency container of your own snack food
→ Take the chance to chat to the class
→ If it is at all familiar to them, end 'break' with Brain Gym - a simple cross crawl to music
→ And at the end of time, get to the door, ensure the room is tidy, and take your leave of them as they go out
→ Quick spray with air freshener (the room, not us!)
→ Loo visit
→ Be prepared to make allowances if the class we next teach hasn't had such a positive experience in their break …

In my last school as a form tutor, tutor groups returned to bases during wet breaks, and this gave me the chance to catch up with several students that hadn't been possible during the normal routine of the day. Although I had yet to encounter such techniques as HeartMath, these sessions were productive and enjoyable for all of us, and enabled me to get to know my tutees much better. I didn't look forward to the prospect of losing a break, but with goodwill on both sides, the experience left us all more prepared for the next lesson.

and another thing ...

By now you're probably realising that your own personal quest for peace in teaching will have an enormous knock-on effect on many areas of school life, right down to wet breaks.

Unless we are able to work in a way that will start to change pupils' preconceptions of education, we will not be maximising the chances we have to enable them to prosper. I'm sure the 18th century poet and visionary William Blake would not object to the following adaptation of his 'Garden of Love', originally criticising organised religion.

> I went to the garden of love
> And saw what I never had seen
> A school was built in the midst
> Where I used to play on the green
>
> And the doors of this school were shut
> And 'Thou shalt not' writ over the door
> And teachers in gowns were walking their rounds
> And binding with briers my joys and desires

Without wishing to be too melodramatic, there are still elements of this in the ways in which some schools approach the children and young people who are depending on them for the 'main chance' in life to build the educational foundations we all need. It seems odd that the natural state of childhood is one of joyful exploration and discovery, but that when 'formal' education starts this can become an experience of frustration, failure, humiliation and an unhappiness that communicates itself in challenging behaviour. And perhaps a timely warning comes to all teachers, who have wearily packed away their toys, from George Bernard Shaw:

> We don't stop playing because we grow old; we grow old because we
> stop playing!

Whatever a pupil's earlier experiences (in life as well as school) have been, if we can approach them, peaceful in ourselves, secure in our supportive relationships and confident of our own expertise and educational outlook, much good can still be done, whether in lesson time or during the third wet break of the week.

New beginnings - and endings

Just as you stand at the door of your room to greet the arrival of each new class, and end each session in a similar fashion, then, on a whole school basis, staff can exercise care and control as pupils enter the school at the beginning of the term/day, and when they leave, for either home or a holiday.

No matter what the management realities of a school structure are, for many pupils (and their parents) the head teacher is the most 'important' member of staff, and their presence at any school function sets the seal on it for many of those attending. If we now think of the school as a whole community, the physical presence of the head, together with a cross-section of staff, standing at the school main entrance at the start of the new term, or even every day, makes a powerful statement on several levels:

Similarly, when a selection of staff is present as pupils leave at the end of the day, it sets the tone for the next day;

We may still have to carry out other 'duties', whether to supervise the buses, check that designated areas of the building are now clear and so on: but all of these are held by the presence of the staff who are there purely to 'meet/greet/ take leave'. It is these staff who will provide the message to all pupils that the school values them, and wants them to feel safe and secure - and the presence of such staff in a highly visible way is reassuring to the community too. *"It's a chance for parents to grab a quick word and it helps set the tone"* are the words quoted from one head teacher in an article on 'visible leadership' in the *TES* of 1.11.13.

Yes: there will always be other stuff needing attention, and some of this might still be involving direct contact with individual pupils. But the ten minutes or so these beginnings and endings take will be repaid by hours saved on issues that arise when a school community is not seen as a coherent whole, valued from the head - down? Up? But certainly, valued by us all and, increasingly, by most pupils.

The social impact of being a peaceful teacher

A LIFE RAFT

Schools can undoubtedly become the focus of security for many pupils who, left to their own communities, may be feeling exposed, unsupported, or worse. I have no wish to be judgmental, for families find themselves in difficulties for a range of reasons that are complex, unfair, and cannot be easily 'fixed'. A statement from the charity *Action For Children* firmly reinforces this:

> But whatever the reason for a child suffering neglect, blame is not
> part of the solution.

However, for us as school staff, the effects of this kind of difficulty on our individual pupils can be dire, from hungry, unwashed and tatty youngsters who are soon the targets of bullying and isolation, to those who have become so hardened by hard knocks and failure that the only 'language' they know is one of challenging bravado, of *"Hit first before you are hit - again"*.

BRINGING PEACE TO SCHOOLS

No amount of hand-wringing and social analysis will alter this daily reality, but if schools - in other words, we as teachers, who are sufficiently secure in own personal well-being - can seize the opportunities presented by having these pupils in our classes, then their learning outcomes, and life opportunities, will be vastly enhanced.

By adopting and adapting the suggestions I've made in Section Five, all our pupils will increasingly feel 'held' by the school, which will become even more of a secure base for them. They will come to feel that:

- ✓ They are respected
- ✓ Their needs are acknowledged
- ✓ They are safe in class, around the school, at breaks and during dinners
- ✓ Teachers are kind
- ✓ Their parents are also supported by teachers, who are keen to encourage and help

My last point in this section is one that I acknowledge could well produce the response:

> "But I didn't come into teaching for this - I'm not a social worker - and how will this improve my target grades? And when can I find the time ... ?"

SO - WHY DID WE COME INTO TEACHING?
→ Because we want to help a child or young person reach their potential?

→ Because we like children or adolescents?

→ Because we have a genuine love for our subject that we want to share with our students?

→ Because we want to make a difference?

These valid reasons have to be underpinned by what I referred to earlier as the 'Art, Craft and Science' of teaching (p.133) - good intentions on their own simply aren't sufficient. And the 'science' of teaching, of learning, has demonstrated time and time again that for a child to learn effectively they have to be physically nourished and emotionally secure. Sir William Booth's approach through the work of The Salvation Army was underpinned intuitively by this - feed their bodies first, then save their souls! This too is firmly at the basis for the 'proper breakfasts' that are a feature of Charlie Taylor's school (*TES* 22.7.11).

We're *not* social workers - too true! The unfortunate division that institutionally exists between education and social care does no-one any favours, but is too big a windmill to tilt at here. We simply have to live with the realities of change and crisis in each sector, but try to ensure, to the best of our ability, that we don't unwittingly perpetuate social division and social isolation for families who are struggling to keep their heads above the water.

Here's an example of the difference I think peaceful teachers can make. The tone of a phone call to a single parent whose child has now turned up for the third day in trainers could result in goodwill, or a reinforcement of all the negativity the parent encountered when they were at school themselves ...

"It's Mr Smith here from St Splodge Academy. I'm phoning about Steven's trainers. It's the third day now he's been to school in them, and I am sure you know from the uniform list we sent home at the end of last term, these are not acceptable footwear. I really must

insist that he comes to school properly dressed, and that he obeys our uniform code. Otherwise, we will be looking at a suitable punishment, and I know you won't want that after what happened last term ..."

"Hello, Mrs Drew? It's Mr Smith here, Steven's new form tutor at school. I'm just phoning round at the beginning of term and want to say how pleased I am that Steven has been on time every morning this week. It's great to see that he has a bag too - it's really helping him get organised! And talking of organisation, I'm about 99% certain he won't have given you the uniform letter sent home at the end of last term. It's just that Steven is wearing trainers, and the letter did ask that all pupils wear black shoes. Any chance at all of him getting a pair at the weekend?"

Perhaps both phone calls are a little stereotypical, but there's enough in each to show how we can contact families in ways that stand a chance of a positive outcome, rather than increased agitation. And that 'we' could equally be a member of the support staff, head of year or whoever.

We can too easily switch to an unthinking 'default' setting if we lay the blame for a child's behaviour on their upbringing. But a moment of calm reflection will show that this does nothing to resolve a problem, and if embodied in our subsequent dealings with a family, can make matters far worse. It is a sobering experience to talk to a child in care, who has been removed from an abusive background of neglect and trauma, to hear them say that they would rather still be living back home *"with me mum".* We ignore this profound link, this attachment, at our peril, and need to be able to deal compassionately and positively with families if we wish to avoid further problems with their children.

SCHOOL AS A SECURE BASE

Our target grades *will* be improved if our pupils are able to work effectively, if they find school secure and peaceful. And there is more than enough evidence to show that effective learning happens when children are enabled to access every part of their brains in a relaxed, stimulating environment, free from excess stress and worry. We have already seen how the organisation of an individual classroom can go a long way in achieving this, but there is always more that a whole school approach can achieve, especially if undue tension between home and school is minimised.

Yes, there are only 24 hours in a day! But within this restriction, we can control certain allocations and usage of time, and this is a control that can be more successfully managed if we have positive and realistic expectations of what we can achieve. If all else is ticking along in our own corner regarding a peaceful life, a well-run classroom environment, and if there is something of a wider approach embraced by the school, the knock-on effect will be more co-operative and less challenging pupils. This in turn will release time for the phone call we have just rehearsed, which should release more time and so on and so on …

What we are trying to achieve here is a message to the pupil - mostly subliminal - that in the sense that I described on p.4 and have referred to previously in this book: *"You are held"*.

We are saying to our pupil, to him, or to her, here is a situation in your life where you can feel secure, where *all* the significant adults in this school are concerned for your well-being and are 'looking out for you', and where you can relax and feel accepted.

Because if we don't build such a liferaft for our pupils, especially the troubled and traumatised children and young people, their need for one may be so great that others already there before us will provide one instead. They are the gangs that will give a sense of belonging, acceptance, protection and 'brotherhood' - but at what price!

It's likely that we came into teaching out of a sense of strength, out of a feeling that because of our concerns and passion for life we could make a positive impact on the lives of children and young people. There is every reason why this should still be the case, and every evidence that many of those we influence every day desperately need the security and peace in their lives that we can provide.

Section five

In summary

★ There is much that can be achieved by us as individual teachers working on our own, working from the principles explored in Section One. However, once we start to feel the benefits of looking after our own well-being, our own sense of peace and security, then we will get talking, supporting, encouraging ... and the knock-on effect for the whole school will richly benefit all staff and pupils.

★ If this is further supported by a secure and supportive head teacher, the possibilities for whole school growth are endless. 'Top down - bottom up' is one model, but so too is 'Centre of the circle out to the periphery - and back', when at the centre is the least experienced NQT who is practising peacefulness and the periphery the head: and, a moment later, their positions are reversed, with each mutually supporting the other.

SCHOOL AS A SECURE BASE

* Some of the areas that will enhance and strengthen the whole school include:

→ Support groups
→ The re-organisation and re-appraisal of duty
→ Teachers present and highly visible at key times in the day/week/term
→ Reflecting on our social impact and how we communicate with parents

* If we have high expectations of our school communities, then nothing less than whole school approaches will deliver. We can achieve much as individual teachers; but the sum total of all our efforts, shaped and supported by the head teacher, will always be greater than the parts working in splendid isolation.

Section six
BACK TO THE BEGINNING

So - we stand at the school gates and look back at everything we've achieved.

The pupils have left for the day, with our good wishes and expectations of a welcoming tomorrow echoing in their ears. The playground behind us is litter-free, and the benches, gazebos and trees throw their lengthening shadows across the buildings behind them. Inside, the corridors are peaceful, with the last notes of today's music - Mozart, maybe - playing through the PA system. Colours, sounds, and a general ambience of calm seem almost at odds with the youthful energy that was until a few minutes ago pulsing through each room, and along each corridor. We enter the staffroom, preparing for the meeting a little later with our support group, but before then time for a coffee, a chat and a laugh with colleagues - friends - who are already there.

None of the above is impossible. With goodwill, courage and determination, such an experience could mark the end of each school day.

If we return to the school gates though and look for a quick moment at what's happening beyond, it's still possible to feel dismay at how our educational world can be buffeted by forces seemingly beyond our control. In October 2012, in the space of a couple of weeks, I noted the following points.

- New school building was going to be limited in scope and size, with far more utilitarian standards setting the benchmark for new designs (*The Guardian Weekly* 5.10.12).

- The attainment gap between looked after children and the rest of their cohort at Key Stage 4 was getting bigger, and although their general educational outcomes were improving, OFSTED questioned the worth of Virtual Heads - expecting that in the three years or so of the scheme being initiated, Virtual Heads, and their staff, would be able to turn around decades of under achievement (*TES* 19.10.12).

- 'The reality is that good teachers don't just teach. They care passionately about all the other things. Contacting parents, writing their own letters, working in holidays, doing cover, doing duties - it's part and parcel of the profession' (*TES* 12.10.12). Words spoken by Geraint Jones, the new director of education at Cognita, part of the changing face of the academy movement in English education, pointing to a renewed expectation of our role. True, many teachers do much of this already, but many of the safeguards concerning teachers' conditions of service (their pay and pensions, their length of holiday and working week), that have been used by colleagues who feel under threat from excessive demands and workload, are being whittled away daily by contracts presented to them in the 'new' schools (academies) in which they are now teaching.

And in 2013, an increased emphasis from OFSTED has been on the role teachers should be playing on a broader societal stage:

> It (the programme *Achievement for All*) sets up tailored partnerships between trained coaches, school leaders, teachers and parents and has a strong 'holistic' focus on improving wider school outcomes.
>
> *Unseen Children* 2013a, p.62

> It is evident that the harm that children can suffer from living in families with complex problems cannot be prevented by the social care system alone. There must also be a coordinated response from a range of services, including health, police, schools, national policy makers and communities themselves. Together, they must create an environment that supports and nurtures families and challenges and intervenes to prevent unacceptable behaviour.
>
> *OFSTED Annual Report on Social Care* 2013b, p.10

Both of these official pronouncements are also echoes of what Sir Michael Wilshaw spoke about when interviewed by *The Guardian* on June 14th, 2013:

> Most parents that I've met love their children, but some find it difficult to support their children in terms of educational provision and support at home ... I think then it's the responsibility of schools to intervene very quickly and ensure they become surrogate parents for those children.'

He conceded that put pressure on teachers ...

SCHOOL AS A SECURE BASE

Every teacher matters

So at the end of the day, what are we actually left with? It has to be the deep understanding that we teachers matter. That whatever might come our way from governments, exam reforms, revised curricula, changes to pensions and so on, for schools to work well for pupils, our well-being is paramount, and it can be nurtured in many of the ways I have already discussed, regardless of what else might happen.

Happily, since I started writing this book, I've noticed others also beginning to comment on the growing realisation that our well-being is central to creating an educational environment that will protect our most vulnerable pupils, and enhance the life chances of everyone. Daniel Goleman was interviewed by the *TES* on 22.11.13 for the launch of his new book 'Focus', in which he advocates the importance of mindfulness and applied meditation (which he calls 'attention training') for all pupils. As part of the interview, he ruminated on how teachers, in order to be empathic and caring, "*... have to first manage your own worries, because when you're distracted, you can't pay full attention to your students*". When asked if teachers therefore needed the same training in handling emotions, and in meditation, as their students, Goleman replied "*... I think teachers should demand it, absolutely. With meditation, your ability to concentrate increases at a neuro level. And it turns out that that circuitry is entwined with your brain's capacity for managing emotion*".

Such ideas are also powerfully emphasised in the new book by Louise Bombèr and Dan Hughes, *Settling to Learn* (2013). In their advocacy for troubled pupils, and the pupils' need to first and foremost have truthful, realistic relationships with key adults in their schools, Bombèr and Hughes acknowledge the crucial importance of schools becoming secure bases:

The capacity for healing will increase in its momentum when the pupil
is in a school which provides a safe and secure relational context ...

p.259

As I discussed in Section One and throughout this book, such a process can only
come about once teachers and other key staff embark on a voyage of personal
self-discovery:

Once we're clearer about our own histories and how they have
impacted on us, then the more available we will be to communicate
full acceptance to those pupils in our care.   *ibid* p.116

And such self-discovery is further detailed:

Those of us who are developing mindfulness of what is going on
inside us at body, heart and mind levels in the 'here and now' are
enhancing the likelihood that we'll be able to inhibit our responses
when they are more reactive than constructive.   *ibid* p.305

In a very real sense, it is this reactive response to situations in school, whether
they are challenging pupils, challenging colleagues, challenging new initiatives,
challenging parents or challenging inspectors, that leave us flooded with cortisol,
a flood that can toss us up exhausted and cynical on the shores of despair. So
I've been encouraging you to challenge yourself on this reactivity - by placing
your own well-being firmly in the centre of everything that might happen in
your school. The image I used in the Introduction is worth repeating here.

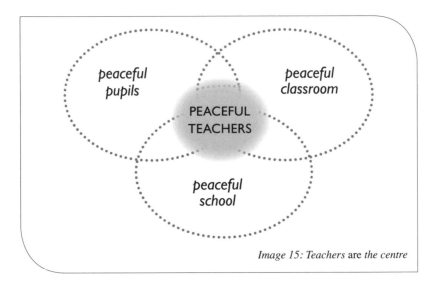

Image 15: Teachers are the centre

Whether you are a lone voice in starting to pursue a peaceful way to making your daily working environment secure and safe for all those in it (including yourself), or part of a network in your school, there is advice and help increasingly available.

As teachers, we are absolutely central to any success our children and young people are going to enjoy, and our inner strength underpins all our efforts to achieve this. The creation of The Peaceful Schools Forum (*see* p.190) will enable us to continue to grow and share our successes, and can be used by anyone who is genuine in their attempts to place their own well-being in the centre of their professional lives.

As the last bell of the day rings, I wish you all success and peace as you look forward to tomorrow.

Good - that went well! Now - must just get that e-mail to Darren's form tutor - oh - wait a minute, that's Jenny! Great - we're meeting later for a drink and our monthly catch-up session, so I can share that with her then. Thinking about it, she's done some good work with Chloe too - wonder if she can throw any light on this make-up business - perhaps we could have a chat with Chloe together some time? Right - just water that plant - a bit near the radiator, but it helps a drab corner. That marking can wait until tomorrow - just tidy up that display for five minutes and then I have that meeting with Simon who is going to support Craig for the next few weeks - it'll be great if he can get alongside Craig as the lad desperately needs someone to trust after all that stuff that happened before he came into care. Grief - it's a bit too quiet in here now! Think I'll put some music on ... oh yes, and a coffee!

Appendix 1

RESOURCES

VISIBLE LEARNING PLUS (™)
This is largely based in Australia, though access to its website does provide a good idea as to how this programme works. In the UK, training in the techniques of Visible Learning is handled by Osiris Educational in a variety of training courses, including a Foundation Course led by John Hattie.
See www.osiriseducational.co.uk

BASE®Babywatching UK
The website contains full details of the recent growth of BASE®Babywatching in the UK, including guidelines as to how you can establish a group in your school, and the training opportunities available. There are also very helpful links to the parent German site set up by Dr Karl Heinz Brisch, the founder of BASE®Babywatching, in a good English translation.
See www.base-babywatching-uk.org

HeartMath®
The UK site gives a good overview of HeartMath®.
See www.heartmath.co.uk
The American site goes much further, and has a very detailed explanation of the educational applications of HeartMath®.
See www.heartmath.org
On YouTube, there are many clips concerning HeartMath®, but of particular interest is the one filmed in a primary school in County Durham.
See *HeartMath and Stress Relief UK School* by Dr Anand

The Hawn Foundation
Full details of the UK MindUP programme are given on this site, together with useful links to Mindfulness in an education setting.
See www.thehawnfoundation.co.uk

Metacognition
Optimus Education, on their web site, host interesting guidelines as to how metacognition might be used in the classroom to aid thinking and learning. Two papers are of particular interest:
Learning for Transfer: Activities for developing an 'inner voice' to monitor thinking, March 9, 2010, and *Learning for Transfer: Hugging and Bridging,* March 23, 2010.
See www.optimus-education.com
Once on the home page, enter 'Metacognition' in the search box.

Appendix 2

PEACEFUL SCHOOLS FORUM

Peaceful Schools Forum

The idea of this Forum is to enable teachers and all other interested individuals to share comments, observations and supportive ideas on the themes raised in this book. This could include constructive criticism, but also ways in which the contributor has approached the notion of 'peace' in their own teaching. It is equally the forum for anyone who wishes to make a start, but is feeling isolated, or for anyone who is looking for support for any other reason.

Registration is free and quick. You should note that the site is moderated, and therefore there might be a slight delay between comments being posted and them appearing on the Forum.

The address is: http://peacefulschools. freeforums.org/

Appendix 3

REFERENCES

Bada, H. et al (2012) Protective factors can mitigate behavior problems after pre-natal cocaine and other drug exposures, reported in *Pediatrics*, December 2012, Vol 130 American Academy of Pediatrics: Illinois

Batmangheldjh, C. (2007) *Shattered Lives* Jessica Kingsley Publishers: London & Philadelphia

Batmangheldjh, C. (2013) *Mind The Child* Penguin Books: London

Beynon, A. (2003) *Standing on Common Ground* MSc in Counselling Studies, Bristol University

Blatchford, P. et al (2009) *Deployment and Impact of Support Staff Project* DCSF - RB 148, August 2009: London

Boddy, D. (2012) *Mind Your Head* John Catt Educational Ltd & The Society of Heads

Bombèr, L. (2007) *Inside I'm Hurting* Worth Publishing: London

Bombèr, L. & Hughes, D. (2013) *Settling to Learn* Worth Publishing: London

Bowlby, J.B. (1969) *Attachment (Vol 1 of Attachment and Loss)* Hogarth Press

Brett, D. (2005) *Protocol to Establish Effects of Peak Performance Training on a Group of Students Statemented with AD(H)D* Hunter Kane: London

Burkett, M. & Daly, J. (2010) *Plants in the Classroom can Improve Student Performance* University of Technology, Sydney: Sydney

Burkett, M. (2010) *Greening the Great Indoors for Human Health and Well-being Project* NY 06021 University of Technology, Sydney: Sydney

Campbell, D. (2002) *The Mozart Effect for Children* HarperCollins: New York

Campbell, D. (1997) *The Mozart Effect* Avon: New York

Campbell, F. (2008) *Good Graffiti, Bad Graffiti Environmental Campaign* (ENCAM): Wigan

Carline, B. (2008) *What Pupils Really Think About Their Schools* Continuum: London & New York

Childre, D. & Martin, H. (1999) *The HeartMath Solution* Harper: San Francisco

Cohen, I. & Goldsmith, M. (2002) *Hands On: How to use Brain Gym in the classroom* Edu-Kinesthetics: Ventura, USA

Cunningham, E. (2011) *Kick the Clutter*, reported in Healthspan, November 2011 Healthspan Ltd: Guernsey

Dennison, P. & Dennison, G. (1990) *Edu-Kinesthetics in Depth, The Seven Dimensions of Intelligence* Edu-Kinesthetics: Venture, USA

Department for Education (2012) *Teachers Standards*, revised June 2013 DFE - 00066 - 2011

Derrington, C. & Goddard, H. (2008) *Whole-Brain Behaviour Management in the Classroom* Routledge: London & New York

Devecchi, C. & Rouse, M. (2010) An exploration of the features of effective collaboration between teachers and teaching assistants in secondary school, reported in *Support for Learning*, Vol 25, Issue 2, May 2010 NASEN: Tamworth, Staffs, UK

Frankl, V. (1959) *Man's Search for Meaning* Rider Press: London, Sydney, Auckland, Johannesburg

Freiburg Research Centre for Occupational and Social Medicine (2013) *Report on the Second Regional Peer Learning Activity of the ETUCE Project* European Trade Union Committee for Education: Brussels

Fullan, J. (1997) *The Challenge of School Change* IRI/Skylight Training and Publishing: Illinois

Geddes, H. (2006) *Attachment in the Classroom* Worth Publishing: London

Gimbel, T. (2005) *The Healing Energies of Colour* Gaia Books Ltd: London

Goleman, D. (2002) *The New Leaders* Sphere: London

Gutkowska, J. & McMann, S. (2000) Oxytocin is a cardiovascular hormone, *Brazilian Journal of Medical and Biological Research*, Vol 33 (6) 625-633

Hannaford, C. (1995) *Smart Moves* Great Ocean Publishers: Arlington Virginia

Hannaford, C. (2002) *Awakening The Child Heart* Jamilla Nur Publishing: Hawaii

Hanson, G. (2012) *Ritalin and Cocaine: The connection and the controversy* The Genetic Learning Center, The University of Utah: Utah

Hattie, J. (2008) *Visible Learning* Routledge: London & New York

Hinde, E. (1997) School Culture and Change: An examination of the effects of school culture on the process of change *Essays in Education*, Vol 12, Winter 2004: University of Arizona: Arizona

Holladay, S. (2012) *Playing with Posture* Hite: London

Hughes, D. (2012) *It Was That One Moment ...* Worth Publishing: London

Hunter Kane (2006a) *High Performance in Education* Hunter Kane Ltd: London

Hunter Kane (2006b) *Peak Performance in Education* Hunter Kane Ltd: London

Hunter Kane (2006c) *The Effects of Peak Performance Training on a Group of Students Statemented with AD(H)D* Hunter Kane Ltd: London

Huxley, A. (1944) *Time Must Have a Stop* Harper and Brothers Publishers: New York

Jersild, A. (1955) *When Teachers Face Themselves* Teachers College Press: New York

Lawrence, D. (1913) Last Lesson, in *Love Poems and Others* Duckworth & Co: Covent Garden, London

Lloyd, A. (2007) The HeartMath® system improves cognitive efficiency and behaviour: a new treatment for ADHD, reported in *The British Journal of Research in Special Needs*, Autumn/ Winter 2007/2008 Blackwell: Oxford

Maslow, A. (1966) *The Psychology of Science* Joanna Cotler Books: New York

Murray, L. (2012) *Calm Kids* Floris Books: Edinburgh

O'Connor, T. (2005) Pre-natal anxiety predicts individual Ddifferences in cortisol in pre-adolescent children *Biological Psychiatry*, 2005, Plenum Publishers: New York

OFSTED (2011) *Excellence in English* Manchester

OFSTED (2013a) *Unseen Children* Manchester

OFSTED (2013b) *Social Care Annual Report* Manchester

Omer, H. (2011) *The New Authority* Cambridge University Press: Cambridge

Pearce, C. (2009) *A Short Introduction to Attachment and Attachment Disorders* Jessica Kingsley Publishers: London & Philadelphia

Pelham, W. (1999) The NIMH Multi-Modal Treatment Study for Attention Deficit Hyperactivity Disorder: Just say yes to drugs? Reported in the *Canadian Journal of Pyschiatry*, 44.10 (1999): 981-990 Ottawa, Ontario

Perry, A. (Ed) (2009) *Teenagers and Attachment* Worth Publishing: London

Renwick, F. & Spalding, B. (2002) A Quiet Place Evaluation, reported in *Inclusive Education Review*, Issue 1, Winter 2003/4 The Department of Education, University of Liverpool: Liverpool

Renwick, F. (2003) A Quiet Place: *Monitoring and Evaluation Report* Department of Education, Liverpool University: Liverpool

Shazer, S. de (1985) *Keys to Solution in Brief Therapy* WW Norton and Co: New York

SCHOOL AS A SECURE BASE

Spalding, B. (2000) The contribution of a "Quiet Place" to early intervention strategies for children with emotional and behavioural difficulties in mainstream schools, reported in *The British Journal of Special Education*, Vol 27, No 3, September 2000 NASEN: Tamworth, Staffs, UK

Strauch, B. (2003) *The Primal Teen* Doubleday: London, Toronto, Sydney, Aukland

Sylvia, C. (1997) A *Change of Heart* Warner Books: London

Teaching Today (May 2012) *The Big Question* 2012 NAS/UWT, Hillscourt Education Centre, Birmingham B45 8RS

Tolle, E. (2003) *Stillness Speaks* New World Library: California

Tomatis, A. (1991) *Pourquoi Mozart* Diffusion Hachette: Paris

World Health Organisation (2001) *Addressing the Links between Indoor Air Pollution, Household Energy and Health* WHO: Geneva

Yardley-Jones, T. & Wesnes, K. (2006) *Cardiac Coherence, Cognitive Function and Enhancing Safety Performance Using The HeartMath System* Hunter Kane: London